Such Language!

To Bill and Jeanne Browning
with big warm friendship
and lots of it. Somebody
else might say it prettier
than that, but they couldn't
say it any truer!

Otto Whittaker
4/15/69

Such Language!

by

Otto Whittaker

DROKE HOUSE, Publishers

ANDERSON, S. C.

Distributed by
GROSSET & DUNLAP
51 Madison Avenue, New York, N. Y.

8375-6730-0

SUCH LANGUAGE

Copyright © 1969 by Otto Whittaker

First Edition

Standard Book Number: 8375-6730-0

Library of Congress Catalog Card Number: 68-28779

Published by DROKE HOUSE, Publishers
Anderson, S. C.

MANUFACTURED IN THE UNITED STATES OF AMERICA

Book Design By Lewis N. Schilling, Jr.

To my wife,

Frances Conrad Whittaker

"She is mine own, and I as rich in having such a jewel as twenty seas, if all their sand were pearl, the water nectar and the rocks pure gold."

— Wm. Shakespeare

Foreword

or,
as the
Revivalists
of Learning
would have
said, and
did,

Preface:

How The English Language Happened

Words began the first time two or more individuals agreed, consciously or unconsciously, that a certain sound made with air from their lungs should stand for a certain thought.

Until writing was invented, these primitive words were engraved on the wind, lost forever to history.

As a result, the earliest language we know anything about is one we really know nothing about. We only guess at it.

But the guess is a highly educated one, as logical as any hypothesis can be, and if the best linguists of the past 150 years have put an abiding faith in it, who can do less? Here's the story:

Somewhere between the Baltic Sea and the Iranian Plateau, some 4,000 to 5,000 years before Christ, there lived a people whose language philologists have reconstructed by sifting out the common denominators of its known descendant tongues. This is the mother-tongue sometimes called Indo-Germanic and Proto-Indo-European, but perhaps best known simply as *Indo-European.*

1

In time, the people who spoke this prehistoric language split into groups and began the centuries of stop-and-go migrations by which their descendants gradually peopled the land from northeast India to westernmost Europe.

Their once-common language, as it was hauled across time into different climates, topographies, and ways of life, and through assorted path-crossings and in-breedings, underwent countless variations and re-variations in sound, grammar and meaning. As a result, words descended from the Indo-European mother-tongue slowly shaped up into related but distinctly different daughter-languages, just as the people who spoke them shaped up into related but distinctly different "nationalities."

Today we know of ten of these basic Indo-European daughter-languages:

Germanic	Tocharian
Hellenic	Indo-Iranian
Italic	Balto-Slavic
Celtic	Albanian
Hittite	Armenian

The Germanic

As men continued to divide into new tribes and nations, most of these basic daughter-languages produced language families of their own — sub-languages which, as different as they were, bore family resemblances easily perceived by language students today.

As English-speakers, we're principally interested in the daughter-language sometimes called Gothonic, Proto-Germanic, and Common Teutonic, but simplest known as *Germanic.*

This was the tongue spoken by the people whom the Roman writers named Germani, a warlike and illiterate people whose habitat is believed to have been that region lying between the Elbe and Oder Rivers in what is now eastern Germany.

Since there are no written records of the Germanic, this language, like the Indo-European, is a hypothetical one. But the

2

speculations upon which it is based are especially close to reality, because philologists, in reconstructing it, have had the written records not only of its daughter-languages but also those of its major sister-languages.

The Sound Shifts, or Drifts

In weaning itself away from the Indo-European, the Germanic made striking changes in the sounds of certain consonants and vowels which other Indo-European daughter-languages did *not* make.

We can only guess at the reason or reasons for these changes, and there are assorted guesses.

One is that the people who spoke Indo-European in the Elbe-Oder region very early came into contact with some other prehistoric population, of whose race, culture, or speech nothing is known, and that fraternization influenced the changes.

Another is that the general living conditions of these Germani, radically different from those of the people who spoke, for instance, the Hellenic and Italic tongues, brought different pressures upon their speech habits. Along with this, we can bear in mind that whereas geography gave the Hellenic and Italic peoples much in common, and that whereas their languages enjoyed very early the fixative influence of writing, the language of the illiterate and more isolated Germani was much more at liberty to stray.

The late Dr. E. Prokosch of Yale University, whose *Comparative Germanic Grammar* is a prime authority, advises us not ot overlook the possibility that these sound changes were the result of tribal imitations of the speech peculiarities of various tribal leaders. This is good advice. Who knows how many of us, the Democrats at least, would be saying "raddio" if Al Smith had been elected President? Or "Cubar," "lawr," and "West Virginiar" had John F. Kennedy lived to serve several terms? Man moves in

3

multifarious ways his leaders to copy.

Whatever the reasons for it, the Germanic tongue clearly made three notable changes away from the Indo-European pronunciation pattern:

The Consonant Shift. Without getting involved in the processes by which the speech organs beat air into speech — and, above all, aiming at an explanation that will do "for all practical purposes" — the main features of the Consonant Shift can be stated this simply:

Indo-European		Germanic
b	became the sound of	p
d	became the sound of	t
g	became the sound of	k
p	became the sound of	f
t	became the sound of	th
k	became the sound of	h

These changes took place pretty much one at a time, and over a period of about a thousand years.

Please note that they really were very simple changes not nearly as radical or contrived as they may seem to the eye. For example:

To make the sound represented by *d*, "duh," the tongue, teeth, lips, etc., perform precisely as they do in making the sound of *t* "tuh." The only difference is that *d* calls for a vibration of the vocal cords, while *t* does not. In the linguist's terms, *d* therefore is a *voiced* consonant, while *t* is a *voiceless* consonant. Similarly, *b* and *g* are voiced, while *p* and *k* are voiceless. (The *s* and *z* are particularly good illustrators of this difference. See for yourself. Make the *s*-sound, *sssss*, then bring your vocal cords into play and listen as *sssss*, voiceless, turns into a strongly voiced *zzzzz*. Or say "dose" three times, then say "doze" three times, and notice how your vocal cords get into the act as you make the switch. This voicing is what makes the difference in the pronunciation of the word *excuse* when we ask, "What's your excuse?" as opposed to when we say, "Excuse me").

An understanding of the Consonant Shift helps greatly to clear up camouflaged relationships between many English words and their equivalents in non-Germanic tongues. For example:

Change of *d* to *t* helps to reveal the kinship of:
  Latin and Greek *edo*: English *eat*
  Greek *deka* and Latin *decem*: English *ten*

Change of *g* to *k* helps to reveal the kinship of:
  Latin *ager* and Greek *agros*: English *acre (akre)*
  Latin *genus* and Greek *genos*: English *kin*

Change of *p* to *f* helps to reveal the kinship of:
  Latin and Greek *pater*: English *father*
  Latin *piscis*: English *fish*

Change of *t* to *th* helps to reveal the kinship of:
  Sanskrit *trayas* and Latin *tres*: English *three*
  Latin and Greek *tu*: English *thou*

Change of *k* to *h* helps to reveal the kinship of:
  Greek *kardia*: English *heart*
  Latin *cornu*: English *horn*

(The above may require some amplification. The Latin *c* is hard, the same sound as the English *k*. In the Indo-European, the k-sound was immediately followed by a hard-breathed h-sound. As in the German *ach* — "ock-hhh" — for example. The change of *k* to *h*, then, is simply one in which only the h-sound survived).

Examples of the *b*-to-*p* change are hard to come by. In

5

Indo-European, the b-sound was exceedingly rare, expecially as the initial sound in a word. One of the few but often-cited examples of this change is Lithuanian *dubs:* English *deep.* Lithuanian, incidentally, is especially faithful to the primitive Indo-European features.

The Stress Shift. In the Indo-European, some words were stressed, or accented, on the first syllable; others on the second syllable; still others on the third syllable, etc., without any rhyme or reason.

The Germanic broke away from this, adopting a rigid system by which only the first syllable of any word was stressed (unless the word bore a prefix).

From the word-detective's point of view, the late Otto Jespersen, one of the most looked-up-to of all linguists, considered this Germanic stress-shift much more important than the consonant-shift. As a rule, the main clue to the relationship of words is found in their first syllables. A *variable* stress system, Jespersen pointed out, often concealed the kinship of two related words by minimizing and subsequently losing in one word the very sound that most clearly showed its relationship to the other On the other hand, the *invariable* Germanic system of stressing the first syllable maximized and tended to preserve common denominators of related words. Here's a makeshift example:

Suppose the Germani had had the adjective *kinglike.* Suppose that in pronouncing it, they had not stressed the first syllable but, as the Indo-European might have, the last — i.e. *kinGLIKE.* By aphesis, the dropping-off of unstressed first syllables, the pronunciation might have become *glike.* In that case, when the written Germanic sub-languages came along, the word would have been spelled as it sounded, and we'd have to be pretty knowing today to know that *glike* was the adjectival form of the noun *king.*

The Vowel-Shift. In Indo-European, the major vowels were *a, e,* and *o.* Here again, the Germanic made changes which the other daughter-languages did not make. The *a* heard in the Latin *mater,* for example, became the *o* of the Germanic *modar.* The *e* represented by *cede* became *ae.* Similarly, the *o* of the Latin *octo* became the *a*-sound represented by the English *eight,* i.e. "aight."

6

These consonant, stress, and vowel changes, then — along with the introduction of suffixes (such as the -th of *strength, truth*) and an assortment of minor alterations in grammar and pronunciation — characterize the basic Germanic as it differed so substantially from its sister-tongues prior to the birth of its own three daughters.

The Germanic Daughter-Languages

Some 300 years before Christ, the increasingly populous Germani moved out in all directions — east into the Baltic basin, north into the Scandinavian peninsula, west and northwest into what are now western Germany and the Netherlands and south toward those regions where they locked horns with the Romans.

As a result, the basic Germanic began picking up dialectal differences which gradually divided it into three sub-groups, one of which led to the English language:

East Germanic: This sub-group included *Burgundian, Vandalic,* and *Gothic.* It is now extinct in all these forms, but Gothic, closer to the basic Germanic than any other descendant, was spoken in the Crimea as late as the 17th century.

North Germanic: Also known as *Old Norse* and *Scandinavian,* this sub-group included those early dialects which have developed into modern *Danish, Norwegian, Swedish,* and *Icelandic.*

West Germanic: This is the language family that eventually produced English. It is characterized by two general types, *Hochdeutsch,* or "High German," and *Plattdeutsch,* "Low German." These two terms are topographical references to the two general regions in which West Germanic dialects were spoken, "West Germania" being a land that rises as it goes south from the North Sea to the Alps. Today's standard German is a product of Old High German. Virtually all other West Germanic tongues have come by way of Low German, i.e., *Dutch, Flemish, Frisian,* and *English.*

For an idea of the similarities of some of these languages

consider the following comparison of three Germanic words with their equivalents in English and ten other descendant tongues:

Germanic:	dagoz	fot	tanth
English:	**day**	**foot**	**tooth**
Gothic:	dag-s	fotu-s	tunthu-s
Old Saxon:	dag	fot	tand
Old Frisian:	dei	fot	toth
Anglo-Saxon:	daeg	fot	toth
High German:	tag	fuss	zahn
Low German:	dag	foot	tan
Dutch:	dag	voet	tan
Danish:	dag	fod	tand
Swedish:	dag	fot	tand
Icelandic:	dag-r	fot-r	tonn

The English Language

The Celts were the first residents of England about whose language we know anything.

These people, who also spoke one of the basic Indo-European daughter-languages, earlier had made their home in what is now southern Germany and northern Austria, but at about 1000 B.C. they began an exodus that lasted for centuries and distributed them in all major European lands, including England.

The first wave of Celts arrived in England about 500 B.C. Others followed. Nobody knows what different lands the different waves came from, or how many there were, or how many centuries the occupation was stretched out over. All we know is that when Julius Caesar attempted to invade the island in 55 B.C., there were enough Celtic Britons to turn him back, but not enough when he returned the following year.

The Coming (And Going) Of The Romans

Caesar's occupation of England was a short-lived one. Political pressures were mounting against him in Rome, and his legions scarcely had a chance to look around before he took them away.

For the next ninety years, the Celtic Britons were left to themselves. At the end of that time, Claudius came with an army of 40,000 men, and the island became an official part of the great Roman Empire. It remained that way for the next 350 years, at which time the great Roman Empire declined and fell. Once again, the Roman legions took their departure, this time for good.

Strangely, during all those years as the language of the conquerors, and therefore the language of status, Latin had failed to displace the Celtic tongue.

Jutes, Angles, and Saxons

With the Romans gone, the Celtic Britons were attacked almost immediately by Picts and Scots from the north. Softened by centuries of Roman protection, they called on the Jutes for help.

The Jutes, a small nation of Frisian-speaking people in Jute-land (Jutland) across the North Sea, proved to be more foe than friend. They confiscated Kent for themselves, thus providing a port of entry for their fellow Frisians, the Saxons of Holstein, who took over the remainder of southern England (Sussex and Wessex). Subsequently, a third Frisian people, the Angles of Schleswig, commandeered most of the eastern half of the island.

The Jutes, Angles, and Saxons, wrote Historian John Richard Green, were "drawn together by the ties of a common blood, common speech, common social and political institutions." They also were drawn together by a common ambition for self-improvement, which they gratified by driving the Celtic Britons repeatedly westward, in and out of new homelands, for the next 125 years.

Some of the Britons wound up in Ireland and Scotland; some in Wales; some in those extreme southwestern counties known as West Wales, and some shook the soil of England forever off their feet and crossed the Channel to what is now Brittany, "Little Britain," on the north coast of France.*

*The Celtic tongue they spoke, already divided by dialects, further shaped inself into two general sub-groups: (1) *Gaelic,* including Irish, Manx, and Scots Gaelic or Erse, and (2) *Cymric,* sometimes called *Brittanic,* which is represented by Welsh, Breton, and the now extinct Cornish. The last known speaker of Cornish was an old lady who died in 1777. Welsh and Breton, of course, have survived, and with remarkable fidelity to each other.

They left numerous Celtic place-names for the land (including *London, Thames, Avon, Trent, Kent,* and the *"Cumber"* of *Cumberland*) but only a handful of Celtic words for the coming English language. This is understandable. When the Celtic Britons left, it was an enemy language they took with them. Those few who remained behind were social inferiors, usually slaves bereft of all status, bankrupt of anything worth emulating.

More *-Saxon* than *Anglo-*

The Anglo-Saxon-Jute trinity divided England into seven separate kingdoms, in each of which the prevailing language was that of the ruling member of the trinity.

The Jute tongue developed into what is known today as the Kentish dialect.

The Anglian diverged into two dialects, the Northumbrian and the Mercian.

The Saxon became the West Saxon or Southern English dialect.

(These original "Anglo-Saxon" dialects continued to diverge, resulting in the more than twenty dialects spoken in England today. King's (or Queen's) English, sometimes called London Standard and Standard English, is a derivation of the earlier East Midland dialect, and thereby hang assorted interesting speculations:

Had this standard form come from the Yorkshire dialect rather than the East Midland, today we might be saying "hoo" for *she,* "han" for *have* and "shan" for shall (just as we say "shan't" for *shall not*).

Had it come from the Southern English dialect, instead of *-s* our standard plural ending for nouns might be *-en*, as in *oxen, children, brethren*.

Had it come from the Northumberland dialect our pronunciation of the *r*-sound might be the throaty burr which has earned Northumberland the nickname of "Croakumshire."

Had it come from the dialect spoken in Devon, Dorset and Somerset, which are called "Zedland," meaning "Z-land," we might sing of "red zails in the zunzet."

And had it come from Cornwall we might pronounce *daughter* as "dafter" — which is not so strange when you remember how we pronounce *laughter.*

Wessex, where West Saxon was spoken, was the kingdom of Alfred the Great. Like Charlemagne, Alfred had gathered about him not only a powerful army but also a potent team of scholars. In his capital at Winchester, there was a great scratching of pens as men of letters, including Alfred himself, authored works of their own and translated those of others. As Wessex rose to political and cultural leadership in England, the West Saxon dialect rost with it, becoming the standard literary, i.e., *written,* language of the land.

Except for those in this West Saxon dialect, we have virtually no written records of the original Anglo-Saxon-Jutish dialects of English. Many Anglian and Jutish manuscripts were destroyed in Viking raids, and those that survived were subsequently copied by West Saxon scribes and thus transferred to that dialect. For this reason, the language we refer to today as Anglo-Saxon is considerably more -Saxon than Anglo-.

The Old English
Period (450 — 1100)

Anglo-Saxon had no more chance of remaining "pure" than any other language at cross-currents with other languages For this reason, linguists prefer to call it *Old English,* to represent not just the larval English tongue but also its development under assorted pressures covering a period of some 650 years.

The outstanding feature of Old English was its great growth in vocabulary. With extensive borrowings from other tongues and a remarkable capacity for manufacturing new words, it rapidly grew into what Simeon Potter, in *Our Language,* describes as "the most advanced vernacular in Europe."

This vocabulary expansion was influenced chiefly by three events — the Christianization of the land, invasion by the Scandinavian Vikings, and invasion by the Norman French, in that order.

Latin Christianization

The Christianization of England began about 600 A.D.

As you'd expect, many of the Latin words it brought in were religious terms, such as those which show up in Old English records as *apostol, biscop, nunne, abbud (abbot), munuc (monk), mynster (monastery), scol (school),* etc.

But the linguistically remarkable thing about the Christianization period is the way the Latin presence stimulated Englishmen, not just to adopt Latin words, but also to invent new words from the native stems of their own language. For example, the adjective *manualis,* meaning "of the hand, handy," which Latin had recruited as a noun meaning a small book kept "at hand" — a *manual.* Englishmen accepted the concept, but expressed it in terms of their own, "handbook."

Thus Christianization enriched the language with synonyms. Or over-enriched it, perhaps. In *Beowulf,* the earliest known major English literature, there are eleven synonyms for *boat,* twelve for *battle,* and at least thirty six for *hero-prince.*

The Scandinavian Influence

The Vikings were Danes, Norwegians, and Swedes engaged in a national commerce handed down by their forefathers — pirating.

At about 787 A.D. they began raiding English Coastal communities at intervals over a period of about sixty years.

At the end of that time, the Danes decided to occupy the island permanently, and by 869 its eastern half was largely theirs. For almost a century and a half they traded victories and defeats with the English. By the year 1000 the English were keeping a hold on their land principally by buying the Danes off.

In 1013, Svein of Denmark drove Ethelred the Unready into exile in Normandy and took the throne himself. He died suddenly that same year, and his son, Canute, became king. For the next quarter-century, England was ruled by Canute and the two sons who succeeded him, Harold Harefoot and Hardecanute, in that order. During this time, many Scandinavians arrived and settled down in a relatively peaceful coexistence with the English, and Scandinavian words began working their ways into the language.

Because of the natal similarities of the Anglo-Saxon and Scandinavian tongues, it's hard to say how many words the Vikings and their descendants brought into English. Linguists generally agree that 1,800 would be a realistic estimate.

To these can be added about 450 Latin words which the language had adopted during the Christianization period.

When one considers that some seven hundred years later, Dr. Sam Johnson's dictionary listed only 50,000 words, it can be seen that these Latin and Scandinavian additions formed a considerable percentage of the Old English vocabulary as it existed when William the Bastard sailed against England in 1066.

The Norman French Influence

Canute had packed his wife off to an administrative job in Denmark and married Emma, widow of Ethelred the Unready, In the process, he became step-father of Edward, subsequently known (for his piousness) as Edward the Confessor.

When Hardecanute, as the Anglo-Saxon Chronicle recorded in 1042, "died as he stood at his drink and suddenly he fell to the ground with a horrible convulsion," the people welcomed Edward to the throne "as was his right by birth."

Edward's mother, Emma, was a sister of Duke Richard II of Normandy. Duke Richard was the grandfather of that Norman duke known as William the Bastard. This made Edward and William cousins-once-removed. Genetically, such a connection is a slim one, but when a throne is at stake, it's like a bar of iron.

History may long debate whether Edward promised to name William as his successor in England, but there's no doubting that William somehow had gotten that impression. Accordingly, when

Edward on his death-bed turned the throne over to Harold, whose mother was a relative of Canute's, William began preparations to take what he insisted was his. In October, 1066, he sailed the English Channel, defeated Harold at the history-changing Battle of Hastings, and became the first of four successive Norman kings of England.

As might have been expected, the bastard gave all the good government jobs to Norman Frenchmen.

Also all the good church jobs.

As a result, Norman French became the national law language, the national literary language, and the only language, other than Latin, taught in schools.

> (There was a substantial difference between Norman French and Francien, the dialect which became today's standard French. France was a land of duchies, where dukes were sub-kings and where different dialects were spoken. Francien, known also as Central French, Parisian French, and Ile-de-France, was spoken in regions closer to the Latin Romance influence. The Norman, Picard, Flemish, Burgundian and other French, or Frankish, dialects clung more to Germanic characteristics. Norman French was especially closer to Old Norse (North Germanic), as the name Norman, "North man," suggests).

As the new masters of England, the Normans made no calculated attempt to force the English population to their language. Nor did the English, with few exceptions, make any conscious effort to embrace it. It was there, and it was inevitable that some of its words should rub off on them. But two hundred years after Hastings, when the Middle English period was well under way, less than a thousand Norman French words had adhered to the English vocabulary. The big impact of French on English was yet to come.

The Middle English
Period (1100 — 1500)

In the general scheme of things, the status of a language is exactly proportionate to the status of those who speak it. In Norman England, for some 150 years, the status of Englishmen was exactly zero. At the end of that time, the picture had changed, but only at the expense of two great national misfortunes.

First, King John in 1204 lost Normandy to the Capetian king of France, Philip II. The ties between the Norman English and their French homeland were now snipped. As a result, the Normans drew closer to the native English. When England in 1337 began a long series of hostilities to recover its lost French holdings, union against a common enemy drew them still closer.

Secondly, soon after these wars started, the Black Plague struck England. Death swept the island, killing off at least one-third of the population. It was the poor people who died most. This resulted in a labor shortage and wages went up. Lured by good jobs, the slavelike villeins began fleeing their masters' manors and waves of free peasants followed them.

Meanwhile, a third class of Englishman had been rising, a middle class composed originally of craftsmen and merchants who, collectively and sometimes individually, became very powerful.

The outcome of it all was a great boost in the status of the commoner and his English language. By 1349 English was being taught in a few schools; by 1356 the mayor of London had ordered that all sheriff's court proceedings be carried out in English; in 1362, Parliament legislated the same requirements for all lawsuits, and by 1385 there was scarcely a school that didn't teach English. Meanwhile, literature by men like Chaucer, Wycliffe, Malory, and Lydgate had come along to further establish English as the language of the land, and the East Midland dialect as its standard form.

As English became increasingly prestigious, it also became increasingly Frenchified. As Mario Pei says in *The Story of English,* "As a slave tongue, English kept sullenly to itself. . .as the free tongue of independent men, English was more than willing to embrace French and take it to its heart."

It embraced it to the tune of thousands of French words. In the present-day English vocabulary, there are many easily-recognized French words, such as *maison, risque, belle, rouge, garage, chaise longue, madame, petite, beau,* etc., but there are many, many more whose French blood is seldom suspected. For instance, how many of the following would you say we owe to the French?

mortgage	tax	state	office	exile
tripe	proof	poultry	taste	medicine
cost	satisfy	stubble	firm	squirrel
blame	bailiff	slave	bucket	faith
cry	pain	harlot	galoshes	stew
beef	bar	dean	sermon	easy
latch	porch	pay	air	image
boots	button	cloak	arson	soldier
ambush	awkward	havoc	checkers	supper
stomach	mutton	roast	toast	cellar
pork	alum	poison	copy	sure
nice	rinse	gum	harness	bacon

All of these words came into English via French, and in their variety, give us at least a token idea of the extent to which English-speakers rely upon French borrowings in their everyday communication with each other.

Note, however, that French words — which included a great number of Frenchified Latin words — seldom were adopted to fill a vacancy in the English vocabulary. In almost every instance, English already had a word for the same concept. The French word came in because it was preferred, and then either displaced the English equivalent or survived alongside it long enough for a variance in meaning to occur. The English *hearty,* for example, originally had the same meaning as the French *cordial;* the same can be said of *stench* and *aroma; ask* and *demand; house* and *mansion.*

During this period of vocabulary enrichment, there also were dramatic changes in the grammar department.

All were for the better, and none was a greater blessing than the decline and fall of the inflected endings that once plagued nouns and pronouns and the adjectives that modified them.

These were endings pronounced and spelled in different ways to show whether the main part of the word was (1) nominative, accusative, genitive, or dative in *case;* (2) masculine, feminine, or neuter in *gender,* and (3) singular or plural in *number.* For example, in Old English there were ten different ways to say "this" — *thes, theos, this, thas, thisse, thisses, thissa, thissum, thisne* and *thys* — with strict grammatical rules about which form to use when.

The Middle English period rescued us.

During this period all unstressed vowels came to be pronounced alike. The various sounds of *a, e, o,* and *u,* when they occurred in unstressed syllables, all fell together in one common sound — that of the inorganic *e,* as in *fallen, taken, chosen.* With this, the great mish-mash of inflected endings, robbed of the thing that made them different, fell into disuse and disappeared. Today we have only one all-purpose adjective form, and the only differences in the noun form are the final *s* which shows plural number and the *apostrophe + s* which denotes possession. Instead of ten forms of the demonstrative pronoun *this,* we have only two — *this* and *these.* Hallelujah.

Another Middle English simplification was in verbs. Many strongly conjugated verbs — those which, like nouns, had significantly different endings to denote different forms — disappeared entirely. Many of those which remained fell away from stressed endings and became weakly conjugated, i.e., the differences in their tense and mood forms became weak differences. *Oke,* the past tense of *ache,* gave way to *ached,* for example. Similarly, *clew* became *clawed; rewe* became *rowed; stope* became *stepped; shew* became *showed, yold* became *yielded,* etc. (Some strongly conjugated forms survived, of course, which is why we say *knew* instead of *knowed; blew* instead of *blowed,* and *tore* instead of *teared*).

In Chaucer's day, the characteristic terminal *e* was always pronounced. *Done, bende,* and *frowne,* for example, were pronounced "dun-uh," "bend-uh," and "frown-uh." Later in the Middle English period this terminal stress disappeared, and with this change there came the freedom to use verbs also as nouns. *Kiss, dress, flutter, drain, bid, glance, haul, cut, strike, frown, smile,* and *dismay* are just a few of the legion of nouns which we have drafted from identically-pronounced verbs. Without this change, we couldn't say that a man drives a certain *make* of car, that a prize-fighter takes a *dive,* or that a girl has a good *shape.*

Many Old English words had begun with the sound of *hw,* with a strong bearing-down upon the *h.* During the Middle English period, the tongue eased up on the *h*-sound. With this, *hwaet* became *what; hwaer* became *where; hwo* became *who; hwanne* became *when; hwy* became *why; hwal* became *whale; hwarf* became *wharf; hwetstan* became *whetstone; hwaete* became *wheat; hwil* became *while,* etc.

Other words beginning with *h* followed by a consonant dropped the *h* altogether. Thus *hlystan* became *listen, hreaw* became *raw, hrer* became *rare,* etc.

Another change of the Middle English period was the dropping of the initial *k, g,* and *w* from the sound of certain words, but not from their spelling. This explains the pronunciation of such present-day words as *knee, knead* and *knight; gnaw, gnat,* and *gnostic; wrestle, wright* and *wreak.*

And it was during the Middle English period that *-s* conquered *-eth* as a verb-ending, converting *goeth* to *goes; giveth* to *gives; speaketh* to *speaks,* etc.

Which demonstrateth that the old order changeth.

But despite these and other transitions, English still was English. It had broken a lot of its old habits and submitted to copious transfusions of French and Latin blood, but its character was still as English as kidney pie when history rang up the curtain on the Renaissance and its Revival of Learning.

The Modern English
Period (1500 — — — —)

After almost a thousand years of "the Dark Ages," Europe looked back longingly upon the grandeur that had been ancient Greece and Rome.

With this, the Renaissance was launched.

The Renaissance was "a revival of learning," a massive turning to antiquity to learn the lessons that had built the great Greek and

Roman civilizations. It was no longer enough that those lessons should reveal themselves only to the few who could read Latin and/or Greek. They now had to be delivered up to all men of affairs. To deliver them, scholars from the Tiber to the Thames began translating the Classics and other Latin and Greek antiquities into 16th century languages.

In England, translation promptly exposed the inadequacy of the English language. There simply were Classical concepts for which there were no satisfactory English words. To meet the need, translators began lifting Latin words, anglicizing them as best they could, or would, and turning them loose as full-blown English words.

With this, a great howl went up, touching off a war of words which was to rage for years.

Those who objected argued that these "ink horn terms" were as obscure in meaning as the Latin and Greek from which they were grabbed, and that clarity was being crucified upon a cross of pedantry and artificial scholarship.

"Many English writers have not done so, but using straunge wordes as latin. . .do make all thinges darke and harde," wrote Roger Ascham, the man who had been Queen Elizabeth's tutor.

"Some seek so far for outlandish English, that they forget altogether their mothers language," said Thomas Wilson in *The Art of Rhetoric*. "I know them that thinke Rhetoric to stand wholie upon dark wordes, and hee that can catch an ynke horn terme by the tail, him they coumpt to be a fine Englishman, and a good Rhetorician."

What were the ink-horn terms to which Wilson objected?

Extol, capacity, celebrate, dexterity, fertile, native, relinquish, expend, and *confidence,* to name a few. But remember, while these are perfectly familiar and highly functional words today, in Thomas Wilson's time they were little understood, and certainly of unproven worth, and therefore quite traumatic to many sturdy English souls.

We have to remember, too, that not all the Classicists were sincere, service-minded scholars. Some were self-serving showoffs, combing the Classics like mad scientists, forcing affectations upon the language, shooting from the hip at spellings, misinterpreting word orgins, dreaming up false etymologies, and belittling almost any perfectly good English word for which they'd found a Latin

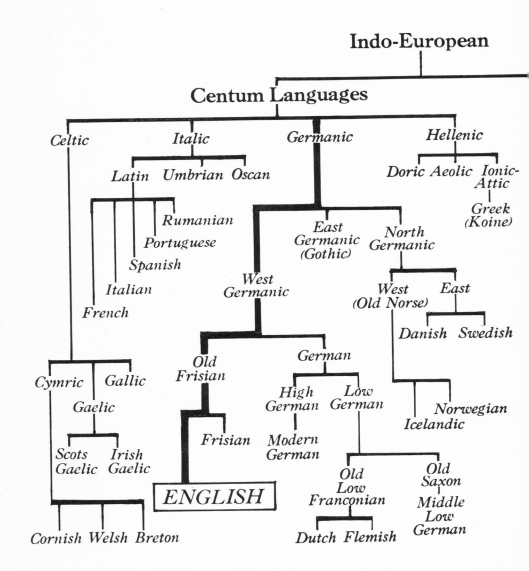

Indo-European

Centum Languages

Celtic   *Italic*   *Germanic*   *Hellenic*

Latin *Umbrian* *Oscan*   *Doric Aeolic Ionic-Attic*

Rumanian   *East Germanic (Gothic)* *North Germanic* *Greek (Koine)*

Portuguese

Spanish

Italian   *West Germanic*   *West (Old Norse)* *East*

French   *Danish Swedish*

Cymric Gallic *Old Frisian* *German*

Gaelic   *High German* *Low German* *Norwegian*

Icelandic

Scots Gaelic *Irish Gaelic* *Frisian* *Modern German*

ENGLISH

Old Low Franconian *Old Saxon*

Middle Low German

Cornish Welsh Breton *Dutch Flemish*

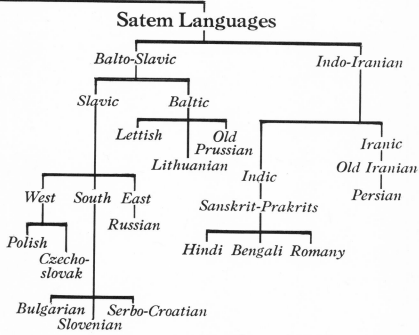

Satem Languages

Balto-Slavic   *Indo-Iranian*

Slavic   *Baltic*

Lettish   *Old Prussian*   *Iranic*

Lithuanian   *Indic*   *Old Iranian*

West   *South*   *East*   *Sanskrit-Prakrits*   *Persian*

Russian

Polish

Czecho-slovak   *Hindi*   *Bengali*   *Romany*

Bulgarian   *Serbo-Croatian*
Slovenian

The first separation of the Indo-European mother-tongue was into two broad groups named for their different pronunciations of *kmtom* or *kentom*, the Indo-European word meaning "hundred." Whereas one group clung to the initial *k*-sound, as in the Latin *centum*, pronounced "kentum," the other converted it into a sibilant, as in the (Persian-related) Avestan *satem*. There were other distinguishing characteristics, of course, but all of them are traditionally represented by one of the two opposing labels, *centum* and *satem*.

Only eight of the ten known Indo-European daughter languages are represented on this chart, the *satem* Albanian and Armenian being omitted because they are minor and have produced no descendant languages of their own. Tocharian and Hittite, *centum* languages, are shown because of fairly recent discoveries indicating that there is more to be known about them. We may know it "soon." Then, again, we may not.

equivalent – which, incidentally, is why some books have *Forewords* while others have *Prefaces*. The evil that these men did lives after them in little outrages which no longer bother us, and which are treated more liberally but less charitably later in this book (see *'island'*).

Shakespeare satirized the ink-horn scholars in *Love's Labour Lost,* and Ben Jonson took a jab at them in his *Poetaster,* putting into Crispinus' mouth a nauseous collection which included *lubrical, oblatrant, furibund,* and *turgidous*. Shakespeare's jest loses some of its cream when we are told that the Bard himself coined *frugal, obscene, reliance, dislocate,* and *premeditated* – all eyebrow-raisers at the time but now perfectly at home in the English vocabulary – and Jonson's nauseous collection becomes much less nauseous when we reason that it also included *spurious, strenuous, retrograde, defunct,* and *reciprocal.*

Thus the new words came – words we recognize today as *genius, area, appendix, submerge, axis, momentum, pollen, maximum, minimum, apparatus, specimen, vacuum, status, series, date, modern, militia, pathetic, obstruction, tantalize, lens, dogma, cerebellum, denunciation,* and others to a grand total of about ten thousand.

It was a harvest not easily won, a reaping not without its absurdities. But it enriched the English vocabulary monumentally, made writers feel freer to invent and express in fresh ways, helped to give a rhythm and sonorousness to both prose and poetry, and must be put high on the list of all-time great contributions to the language.

While the word-stock thus was being improved, grammar and pronunciation were also in ferment, as they always are. The following are the outstanding developments, in those areas, during the earlier stages of the Modern English period:

Thou, thee, and *ye* were scrapped, leaving *you* as the one-and-only second-person pronoun.

The interrogative pronouns *who* and *which* came to be used also as relative pronouns.

The possessive apostrophe came into standard use (except for *its,* treated later in this book).

There was a growing use of *more* and *most* to form the comparative and superlative degrees of certain adjectives and adverbs, e.g., *more common* and *most common* instead of *commoner, commonest.*

To the eternal torment of purists, prepositions received a growing permission to dangle at the ends of sentences.

The order of words in sentences became more formulated. ("If you please," which actually means "if it pleases you," is a survivor of the old order.)

The standardization of spelling was greatly advanced, thanks largely to William Caxton and his printing press.

And "The Great English Vowel Shift," a gradual rearrangement of the long vowel sounds of the Middle English period, was steadily pushing pronunciation to its present-day sound. Here's an example of the shifting pronunciation of vowels, through the Middle English eras of Chaucer and Shakespeare to the present time:

Chaucer	Shakespeare	Present
boat	boot	boot
beet	bait	bite
aboot	aboat	about
bait	beet	beet
bet	bate	beat
bought	bote	boat
abaht	abet	abate.

The Cosmopolitan English

Although English traditionally has used Latin and Greek as storehouses to be drawn upon whenever a new word must be invented, its eagerness and affection for interesting and serviceful words from any and all languages has shaped its vocabulary into the most cosmopolitan the world has ever known. This small biography of the language wouldn't be quite as right without at least a few examples (excluding French and Latin, previously exemplified). Bear in mind that in some cases our borrowed words have come directly from the source language; in others, via other languages which have borrowed before us:

GREEK:
topic, cosmetic, phone, comedy, hormone, telegram, protein, autocracy, agnostic, zone, chlorine, allergy, pause.

CELTIC:
flannel, whisky, plaid, crag, colleen, ass, bin, slogan, tor.

SCANDINAVIAN:
egg, husband, rag, take, skin, root, law, want, steak, window, trust, sly, ski, geyser, floe, fellow, door, thrall.

HIGH GERMAN:
carouse, poker, quartz, plunder, noodle, umlaut, yodel, nickel, waltz, seltzer, cobalt, hamburger, kindergarten, zinc.

LOW GERMAN:
pickle, brandy, yacht, split, gin, skipper, deck, cruise, luck, snap, spool, buoy, skate, booze, brake, kit.

ITALIAN:
cameo, lava, carnival, umbrella, grotto, confetti, soprano, volcano, bandit, regatta, stanza, solo, replica, tempo.

SPANISH:
rodeo, cargo, lime, silo, escapade, tornado, anchovy, cork, vanilla, cigar, bonanza, alligator, bronco.

ARABIC:
harem, mattress, zero, alcohol, orange, almanac, cotton, carat, hazard, alkali, assassin, caliber, algebra.

HEBREW:
ebony, cherub, behemoth, camel, amen, sapphire, rabbi, jubilee.

PERSIAN:
shawl, divan, rook, caravan, bazaar, paradise, tiger, scarlet, taffeta, musk, tiara, naphtha.

24

HINDUSTANI:
bandana, loot, dungarees, cot, jungle, shampoo, bangle, bungalow, pajamas, chintz, gunny (sack).

CHINESE:
pongee, tycoon, kumquat, tea, ketchup, japan, ginseng, tong, kowtow, chow, chow mein, chop suey.

AFRICAN NEGRO:
banana, tote, zebra, yam, banjo, goober, gumbo, jigger, voodoo, gorilla, juke, jazz, zombie, samba, rumba.

AMERICAN INDIAN:
moose, skunk, pecan, terrapin, tomahawk, opossum, calumet, toboggan, sagamore, bayou, moccasin, totem.

PACIFIC ISLANDS:
bamboo, atoll, gingham, orang-outang, mangrove, launch, rattan, taboo, tattoo, ukelele, lei, aloha.

MISCELLANEOUS:
Slavic — *sable, robot, polka, cravat, mammoth, pogrom, silk, tundra, steppe;* Hungarian — *hussar, coach, goulash, paprika, shako;* Turkish — *khan, horde, tulip, fez, coffee;* West Indies — *mahogany, barbecue, cannibal, hurricane, tobacco, potato;* South American — *quinine, llama, tapioca, jaguar, lagniappe (la nape);* Japanese — *kimono, judo;* Mexican — *chocolate, chili, tomato, calaboose.*

The English vocabulary, reckoned at a minimum of 600,000 words, is estimated to be one-fifth Anglo-Saxon/Scandinavian, three-fifths French/Latin/Greek, and one-fifth You/Name/It. Despite its many infusions from other tongues, it is still English, with a character all its own and a vigor and flexibility not possessed by any other Indo-European descendant — indisputably the most phenomenal language this world has ever known.

People who write books about the whats, whys, and whences of words commonly resort to such trade-talk terms as *assimilation, dissimilation, coalescence, metathesis, amelioration, pejoration, epenthesis, colloquialism, metanalysis, lallation, apocope, rhotacism, aphesis, elision, prothesis, apophony,* and a host of other phonetic labels that will scare you if they can, but submit meekly if you stand up to them. One of the aims of this book is to define and illustrate them within the sugar-coating of what I hope you will find to be light-hearted but responsible little "word-essays." As Alfred Hitchcock is wont to say, "We sha' see."

In not very many pages, the preceding has scampered across some 7,000 years. If you'd like to go deeper into the origin and development of the English language, there are numerous authoritative books available to you, as they've been available to me. Samuel Johnson said, "A man will turn over a library to make a book," and this is true. With a great deal of admiration for their makers, all men of learning and dedication, here are the names of the principal books I've "turned over" to make this one:

Language: Its Nature, Development And Origin, Otto Jespersen
Growth and Structure of the English Language, Otto Jespersen
A History of the English Language, Albert C. Baugh
The Story of English, Mario Pei
The World's Chief Languages, Mario Pei
The Story of Language, Mario Pei
The Families of Words, Mario Pei
The Origins and Development of the English Language, Thomas Pyles
The Story of Speech and Language, Charles L. Barber
Our Language, Simeon Potter
The Miracle of Language, Charlton Laird
A Comparative Germanic Grammar, E. Prokosch
Comparative Linguistics, Robert Lord

Etymological Dictionary of the English Language, W. W. Skeat
Oxford Dictionary of English Etymology, C. T. Onions
Origins, The Encyclopedia of Words, Eric Partridge
Dictionary of Word Origins, Joseph T. Shipley
Nouveau Dictionnaire Étymologique, Dauzat-DuBois-Mitterand
The Oxford English Dictionary
Webster's New World Dictionary
Dictionary of Early English, Joseph T. Shipley
Dictionary of American Slang, Wentworth and Flexner
Dictionary of Slang and Unconventional English, Eric Partridge

Classical Dictionary of the Vulgar Tongue, Eric Partridge
A Dictionary of Yiddish Slang and Idioms, Fred Kogos
Words And Their Ways In English Speech, Greenough and Kittredge
The Romance of Words, Ernest Weekley

I should also like to recommend *American Speech: A Quarterly of Linguistic Usage,* published by Columbia University Press, and *Names: Journal of The American Name Society,* State University College, Potsdam, N. Y.

Otto Whittaker
Roanoke, Virginia

'glass'

(which Cinderella's slipper was not)

After the glaciers of the Ice Age bulldozed their ways north and gave the place a chance to warm up, great forest empires spread across the land south of the Baltic.

There, for eons, giant conifers of now-extinct varieties stood and perspired a gummy resin which time fossilized into a hard, brownish-yellow substance.

When man discovered he could make jewelry out of this substance, markets for it developed in various lands, and as it went into those lands it was given various names.

The Arabs called it *anbar,* a word which has wound up in present-day English as *amber.*

The Greeks called it *elektron,* meaning "shiny bright."

The Germani, in whose homeland it was discovered, called it *glasam.* This was the primitive root which went into the Germanic daughter-languages and eventually developed into the Old English *glaes,* Middle English *glas,* and present-day *glass.* It also was borrowed by the Latini, who altered it slightly to *glaesum.*

If you've been telling the youngsters that Cinderella's slippers were glass, you're the victim of a massive mistake. Maybe you'd like to set the record straight:

Cinderella, known to the French as *Cendrillon,* the Italians as *Cenerentola,* and the Germans as *Aschenbrotel,* all meaning "little ash girl," is the best-known folktale in the world. There are more than 500 versions in Europe alone.

The oldest known version is Chinese, dating from the 9th century, and the way the Chinese told it, the girl's slippers were gold.

Tales, of course, get garbled in the telling, especially when they go from one language to another. By the time the story was popularized by the Frenchman, Charles Perrault, in 1697, Cinderella's slippers were *fuere,* or fur.

But *fuere* was pronounced very much like that other French word, *verre,* meaning "glass," and this little twist of the tongue has sent a billion people to their graves believing that Cinderella's slippers were glass.

It's good to know they weren't.

Who wants glass shoes?

'panties'

(the word we owe to a beheaded Christian)

If Galerius, Roman emperor from 305 until 311, hadn't beheaded his friend and family doctor, the girls would have had to find another name for panties.

But off with the doctor's head it was. He did the one thing Galerius couldn't forgive. He became a Christian.

The people of Venice, one of the first strongholds of Christianity, made the martyred doctor their patron saint. They called him *Pantaleone,* meaning "all-lion," i.e., exceedingly brave, and began naming their babies for him.

In time there were so many Venetians named *Pantalone,* the contraction of *Pantaleone,* that the outside world made it a nickname for all Venetians.

Meanwhile, the Venetian theatre invented a new form of comedy in which certain clownlike character always appeared. Until that time, men had always worn skirts or robes, or fig-leaves, but this character wore an odd get-up that began at the waist, came down over each leg separately, and ended with bows just below the knees. Amused, the outside world promptly applied the name *Pantalone* not only to the clownlike character, but also to his breeches.

But the garment had its practical side, and with assorted modifications came to be standard male apparel throughout Europe.

The French called it *pantalon.*

The English adopted the French name, but substituted the augmentive ending *-oon* (just as they did with the French *ballon,* balloon, and *carton,* cartoon). The plural *s* was an inevitable as it was in *scissors, pliers,* and *trousers,* and so *pantaloons* became the common English word for the garment. This was a bit too much for the impatient human tongue, and so in time the word was shortened, and that's the history of the word *panties.*

Of course, this same story could be used to show how we got the name for man's pants. But that seems dull.

'tiger'

(you could hold one in your hand)

What do you suppose we're expected to hold when somebody sings out, *"Hold that tiger!"*?

Put all thoughts of real, live tigers out of your mind.

It was a five-card poker hand, not a four-legged feline, that inspired the jazz classic, *Tiger Rag.*

Although seldom heard today, "tiger" once was a provincial name for the worst possible poker hand. It came over from faro, another card game in which the player has a tiger by the tail when he bluffs on a low hand. Alan Lomax confirms the terminology in *Mr. Jelly Roll,** his biography of "Jelly Roll" Morton:

"And all his life Jelly Roll held a tiger by the tail. In barrelhouse lingo 'tiger' meant the lowest hand a man could draw in a poker game — seven high, deuce low, and without a pair, straight or flush. It takes nerve to hold on to a tiger, and all he had was the music of the Storyville bordellos — it was his tiger and he bet his life on it."

The real tiger, stripes and four legs, was named for its great speed. The word *tiger* comes through Latin and Greek from the Persian *tighri,* meaning "arrow." It's related to the Sanskrit *tigma,* which meant arrow-like in the sense of "flying swiftly." The Tigris river was so-named because it, too, moves swiftly.

The man-eating tiger isn't as fast as the non-man-eating tiger. He's an old, slow tiger. He wouldn't eat men if he could catch anything else. This is humiliating, but facts are facts.

*Written while Mr. Lomax was on the staff of the Library of Congress, quoted by permission of Duell, Sloan & Pearce, Inc., publisher

'Vulgar Latin'

(it was a romantic bastard)

The Old French verb *enromancer,* "to romance," had nothing to do with affairs of the heart. It meant to speak or write in the everyday language, to put it in the vernacular, to say it the way the Roman people would.

This touches on a little question that may have pursued you:

Why are French, Spanish, Italian, and other tongues that came from Latin called "Romance" languages? Why not "Latinate," or at least some designation based on Latin, not Rome?

It's because those languages didn't come from Latin. Not directly, at least.

Latin was the Classical tongue — the precise, rule-ridden language of literature, law, science, and the church — and perhaps, to some degree and for some brief duration, that of the primmest, most proper, and most pedantic of the patrician class.

But "Roman" was the slangy, big-shouldered, big-city Latin. It was the vernacular, it was street language, it was the language to which the Roman legions kept bringing words from other lands. In simplest terms, it was "people talk," and that's just what it was called — *Vulgar* (or *Vulgate)* Latin, from the Latin word *vulgus,* meaning "the common people, the public."

Here's an interesting example of the difference between Latin and Vulgar Latin:

Caput is the Latin word for "head." It is the progenitor of *captain, capital, cap, caption, chapter,* and assorted other words related to heads and headship. But the Vulgar Latin word for "head" was *testa.* Actually, testa was a legitimate Latin word meaning "pot" or "shell," which had captured the public fancy as a slangy way of referring to the human head. The English language has parallels in its own slang-words "bean," "nut," and "noggin."

Testa became the Old French word *teste,* meaning "head." One of its derivations was the Middle French *testu,* "headstrong," which the English language has borrowed as *testy.* Gradually *teste* became *tete,* the modern and completely un-vulgar French word for the head.

It's important to know about Vulgar Latin, because any study of English word origins must deal with the French language, and Vulgar Latin is the big, throbbing vein from which Old French got most of its blood. It had the happy, unfettered, imaginative, blithely belching-out-loud force without which a language soon bores itself to death. It was a bastard language, but a romantic one, serenaded by no less a romantic than Byron:

> "I love the language, that soft bastard Latin,
> Which melts like kisses from a female mouth."

'stark—naked'

(a tale about a tail)

The little wood-warbler known as the redstart loves to spread his tail to show off the reddish-orange markings underneath.

This colorful plumage is the reason for his name. He has a red start, *start* being an obsolete English word meaning "tail." In Old English it was *steort,* from the Old Norse *stertr,* Old Frisian *stert,* all meaning "tail." The Middle English form was *stert,* pronounced "start" just as the Englishman now pronounces *clerk* and *derby* as "clark" and "darby."

This is the *start* in the old expression *start-naked* – literally, tail-naked, or bare-arsed – which we know today as *stark-naked.* And undoubtedly we'd still be saying *start-naked* today, if it weren't for assimilation.

In linguistics, *assimilation* is that phonetic force by which the sound of one syllable is so dominated by the sound of a neighboring syllable that it copies it, thereby losing its own identity. It is literally swallowed up by the stronger sound, or assimilated. A good example of this is the pronunciation of *cupboard,* in which the *p*-sound is swallowed up by the more influential *b*-sound, leaving "cubboard."

When Martin Luther King was assassinated, I heard two newscasters and one cab driver call him Arthur Luther King. With the mind on things other than enunciation, the *th*-sound in *Luther* forced the *t*-sound in *Martin* to copy it, and the mind unconsciously ordered the tongue to convert "Marthin" to the more familiar "Ar*th*ur."

The *k*-sound is an especially notorious assimilator of other sounds. It swallows up the *d*-sound in *handkerchief*, converting the pronunciation to "hankerchief." In *waistcoat*, the *k*-sound (hard *c*, same thing) assimilates the *t*-sound, leaving "weskit." You may at times have heard the name Art Linkletter pronounced *Ark* Linkletter. Here the *k*-sound in the last name reaches over to the first name to swallow up the *t*-sound and install itself in its place. And that's exactly what happened to turn *start*-naked into *stark*-naked. In this particular case, the change was aided and abetted by the purely coincidental meaning of the unrelated word *stark*, i.e., "absolutely," which was a perfect fit for the implication of *absolutely*-naked. Even *Playboy's* photographers, who must be a pretty bored lot by now, will admit that tail-naked is a pretty absolute degree of nakedness.

******

The opposite of assimilation is *dissimilation,* the tendency to change one sound in a word because it is found again in the same word. The tongue simply rebels at enunciating the sound a second time. Especially if the sounds of *r* and *l* are involved. For example, *colonel* comes out "curnel." Dissimilation changed *grammar* to "glammar," prompting Sir Walter Scott to coin the word *glamour,* and the word *purple* originally was *purpre.* Sometimes dissimilation results in the loss of a sound rather than a change, which is why some people say "Febuary" and "Missippi."

'question—mark'

(How did it get in the shape it's in?)

Who decided the question-mark should look as it does?
Why not any of a thousand other shapes?
How did the question-mark come to be, anyway?

It started with the early medieval printers. They fashioned it from parts of the Latin word *quaestio,* meaning a querying, a questing. They took its initial letter and put it on top of the terminal letter, like this:

q
o

That's how the question-mark began, and so it probably would have remained, had it remained in the hands of the printers. But when ordinary citizens put their impatient pens to it, it stopped running true to type. The *q* lost part of its curve and more and more resembled a hook, and the *o* got smaller and smaller until it was only a dot, and that's how it's been ever since.

Much the same thing happened with the exclamation point. The Latin expression *io,* pronounced "yo," was roughly equivalent to our *wow.* Remembering that the earliest *i* was not dotted (as explained later in this book), you can see that *io* provided both the nature and the parts the printers needed. They put the undotted *i* on top of the *o,* and man's hasty hand did the rest.

There are excited questions and questioning exclamations, and in such cases neither the question-mark nor the exclamation point, single-handedly, can do the job. If you were told that some eccentric millionnaire stranger had left you ten million dollars, and wanted to be sure your ears weren't deceiving you, which of the following would you say?

"Ten million dollars?"
"Ten million dollars!"

Obviously, this situation would call for *both* marks — "Ten million dollars!?" — but that's awkward, and one never knows whether to put the question-mark in front of the exclamation point or vice-versa. So the American Type Founders Company has labored and brought forth a solution. They call it the interabang — *intera* for interrogation and *bang* for exclamation — and it looks like this:

$$?$$

The interabang was invented several years ago and is having a hard time catching on. It may be years before you see another one. But that's all right, it may be years before an eccentric millionnaire stranger leaves you ten million dollars.

'cuckold'

(or, How to send a Husband to Heaven)

A cuckold, as this enlightened age well knows, is a husband who has been done wrong by a wayward wife and a male friend.

Not *his* male friend. *Her* male friend.

But cuckolds, if we can believe what Caesar told Tiberio in John Florio's *Second Fruites,* are neither to be pitied nor laughed at. They've got it made. In fact, theirs is the very kingdom of Heaven:

"If he knowe it, hee must needs be a patient, and therefore a martir. If he knowe it not, hee is an innocent, and you know that martires and innocents shall be saved, which if you grant, it followeth that all cuckolds shall obtaine Paradise."

To which Tiberio replied, "Mee thinks, then, that women are not greatlie to be blamed if they seeke their husbands eternal salvation, but are to be commended, as causes of a worthie effect."

This reasoning is highly speculative. Fortunately, we are on surer ground with the origin of the word *cuckold*. It derives from the name and cuckolding fame of the female cuckoo.

Not the American female cuckoo. So far as anybody knows, her morals are impeccable. But the *European* female cuckoo, oh boy. No inhibitions whatsoever. She'll even skip off with some other bird when she's right on the verge of becoming a mama. In Europe, very few baby cuckoos know their father.

36

This explains why Shakespeare, in *Love's Labour Lost*, cries, "Cuckoo, cuckoo; O word of fear, Unpleasing to a married ear!"

The word *cuckold* applies only to males. It seems we don't have a word with the same meaning for females. But it seems we ought to have.

'wittol'

(a special kind of cuckold)

There are three kinds of cuckold:
(1) Those who don't know they're cuckolds.
(2) Those who know they are and don't like it.
(3) Those who know they are and couldn't care less.

For the No. 3 variety, the English language once had a special name — *wittol*. Apparently it came from *witewal*, later *woodwale*, the name of the simple and amiable woodpecker which legendarily hatched the cuckoo's eggs while Mama Cuckoo was out carrying on. Hence *wittol*, a cooperative fellow who stays home while his wife goes to town.

'ampersand'

(Brutus stabbed the wrong man)

Brutus came not to praise Caesar but to stick a knife in his back, and as mighty Caesar went down he said, "Et tu, Brute?" This is history's best-known dramatization of the Latin word *et*, meaning "and."

Now, please consider another Roman of that day, one Marcus Tullius Tiro.

Tiro was Cicero's amanuensis. In that capacity it was his job to write down whatever Cicero dictated, and to make his job easier, he invented this familiar shorthand symbol:

&

For centuries this symbol, also meaning *and,* was known as "the Tironian Sign." And then in England, thanks to the old hornbooks and a schoolroom recitation custom, there gradually emerged a new name, *ampersand.*

Directly after the letter *z* in the alphabet, these hornbooks* usually bore certain other writing symbols, one of which was the Tironian Sign. When pupils stood to recite their ABC's, it was their custom to call special attention to those characters which, by themselves, were also complete words. For this purpose, they used the Latin term *per se,* meaning "by itself." For example, they'd recite, "a, *per se,* a, " " i, *per se,* I," and "o, *per se,* O."

When they'd run the alphabet and come to the Tironian Sign, they called it out as, "and, *per se,* and." These four words gradually coalesced into one, *ampersand.* The change from "andper-" to "amper-" was to be expected. The sound of *n* frequently changes to that of *m* when it's followed by *p;* the words *imperil* and *impassion,* for example, originally were in*peril* and in*passion.*

If this seems complicated, blame it on Tiro. No less that he deserves, for hammering the simple *et* into that twisted and tortured ampersand. Get a pencil and try to make a decent ampersand. Unless you have the hand of an artist or the soul of a saint, you may agree, Brutus slipped the shiv to the wrong man.

---

*Not a *book* as we know books today. The hornbook was a sheet of paper imprinted with the alphabet, the ten digits, certain symbols, and the Lord's Prayer, cemented to a wooden tablet. The tablet had a handle, much like a hand-mirror. For protection, the printed sheet was covered with a thin sheet of translucent horn, hence the name *hornbook.*

'child'

(and how to get a $219,000 jump on the tax man)

According to an old legend, the Countess of Henneburg insulted a beggar who exacted a devilish revenge. He prayed that the Countess should have "as many babies as there are days in the year" — *all at once*. As a result, the Countess on Good Friday, 1276, gave birth to 365 babies.

Now please consider the word *child*, which is almost as full of little surprises as the Countess was.

It comes from the Old English *cild*, a relative of the Gothic word for womb. (In Old English, the consonant *c*, when immediately followed by a front-vowel, took the *ch*-sound, as in *chin*. Hence *cin = chin*, *cicen = chicken*, *cild = child*, etc.).

Although the modern meaning of *child* fits all youngsters from infancy through puberty, the original meaning was strictly that of a baby just born or one conceived but not yet born. That's why we have the word *childbirth* today, but no such word as "babybirth."

At one time, "childing" was applied to human mothers just as "calving" and "foaling" are applied to bovines and equines. A *child bed* wasn't a child's bed, but the bed to which the mother took to have her child. The term *childwife* didn't mean an under-age bride, but a woman of any age who had just borne a child.

In some parts of England, *child* applied only to girl-babies. That's why the shepherd who found Hermione's abandoned baby in *The Winter's Tale* said, "A boy or a child, I wonder?"

A *childwite* was a fine imposed upon any fellow inconsiderate enough to get a bondwoman with child without first getting her owner's permission. And a *childe* wasn't a child at all, but a young man of gentility, usually a candidate for knighthood, such as Byron's Childe Harold. In this case, *childe* meant "well-born," a more purposeful reference to the womb.

Ladies should be hesitant about insulting beggars. But if insult they must, there is one consoling thought. At $600 per dependant, what a jump their husbands will have on the tax man.

'hendiadys'

(a matter of two for one)

"Run and give Daddy a kiss."
"Call and see if Mabel is home."
"You went and told."
"Look and see if the mail has come."
"It's nice and quiet in here."
"Sure is. Gee, you smell nice and clean."
"Thank you. You're so nice and polite."

Each of these sentences is an example of the failing known as *hendiadys*. The etymology of this word gives a clue to its meaning. It is a Middle Latin coinage, based on an old Greek expression, *hen dia dyoin*, meaning "one by means of two."

A hendiadys, then, is a figure of speech in which *one* idea is expressed by means of *two* words joined by "and."

As one has probably guessed by now. If not, one will just have to try and do better.

'infant'

(when does one stop being a baby?)

Why is an infant called an *infant*?

In English, the word goes back to the obsolete *faunt*, which meant "small child." *Faunt* came from the Old French *enfaunt*, which in turn derived from the Latin *infantem*, a compound of *in*, not + *fantem*, speaking. By this etymology we can establish infancy or babyhood as lasting until the little one begins to talk, at which time childhood sets in.

'wench'

(Many a man started out as a girl)

Wench is from the Middle English *wenche,* itself a clipped form of *wenchell.* Now a less than complimentary term for a woman, its original meaning was nothing worse than "infant." *Wenchel,* also spelled *wennchell,* is used in the Ormulum, in the account of Christ's birth as announced to the shepherds. Thanks to its connotation of "weak, tender," the word came to apply to the weaker sex, used for a grown woman much as we use "babe" or "baby" for her today. Later it came to mean a common woman.

Girl once applied to male as well as female, meaning only "small child." It came from the Germanic *gur,* child, which had the diminuitive form *gur-wil,* small child. As late as the Middle English period, *gerle, gyrl* and *girle* meant a child of either sex.

But here again, the concept of tenderness,weakness transferred the word to the older female. Chaucer used *gerl* as the word for a young woman, but also referred to young people of both sexes as *girles.* By 1530, *girle* applied exclusively to all young unmarried women, and by 1668 it had a corollary meaning of maid-servant.

The noun *boy* has always applied to the male. There once was a verb, *boy,* meaning the playing by a boy of a woman's role in the theatre.

'butter'

(a lot of put-on)

If that little old winemaker shipped you a *butt,* he'd send you a barrel holding 130 standard gallons of wine. The word comes from the Latin *buttis,* cask.

Another word from *buttis* is *bottle.* The man who looked after the butts and bottles was the *boteler,* later the *buteler,* and now the *butler.*

You may recall that in *Twelfth Night*, Shakespeare has Maria invite Sir Andrew Aguecheek to "bring your hand to the buttery-bar and let it drink." The buttery-bar was a little shelf on the buttery-hatch, or half-door, where a tankard could be rested. And what was the *buttery*? It was the place where the butts were kept. The word is *butt* + *-ery*, sometimes *-ry*, a common suffix denoting the place of actions, occupations, purposes, etc., as typified by *pantry, nursery, vestry, nunnery, library*.

The buttery was always located in a cool place, so it was a good place to keep the food we know today as *butter*. But it is folk etymology (explained later in this book as *false* etymology) to suggest that *butter* derives from *buttery*, or that the two words are in any way related. Their resemblance is purely coincidental.

Butter traces to the Latin *butyrum*, a relative of Latin *bos* and Greek *bous*, meaning bovine, cow. The Old French equivalent of *butyrum* was *burre*, modern French *beurre*, in which the *t*-sound was lost. The Germanic retained it, as typified by the Old High German and Old Frisian *butera* and Old English *butere*.

Although butter has been known since about 2000 B.C., its use as a food isn't nearly that old. The Burgundians used it as a hair-dressing (causing the good bishop Sidonius Apollinarius to complain, in his writings, about their rancid odor). In Tibet, it is still used for illumination. In Africa, it is still used as an ointment. In the United States, it is still used to put on things, such as bread, potatoes, and weight. If one uses enough of it, he'll put on so much weight that he won't want to do anything except sit around on his wine cask.

the 'manuscript u'

(and why a virgin is called a virgin)

Public buildings are built for the public, the *Des Moines Register* has pointed out, and not just for those who understand "the cvstom of svbstitvting the letter *v* for the rovnd-based letters scvlptvred above entrances."

To understand this "cvstom," one need know only that there was no *u* in the Latin alphabet, and that any found there today result only from the tendency in *manuscript*, "hand-writing," to

42

round off the bottom of the *v*. Called *the manuscript u*, this round-bottomed letter for a long while was treated as a *v*, and then gradually took a sound of its own.

Whereas the *u* arrived late in Latin, the *v* arrived late in English. In Old English the v-sound, when it occurred between two vowels, was represented by the letter *f*. This explains the modern difference in such pairs as *leaf, leaves; bereft, bereaved; half, halves; knife, knives; heft, heave; calf, calving*, and so on.

When the *v* finally made its way into English, it immediately fell into harness with the *u*. For a long while both letters were used indiscriminately to represent either sound. In old texts, for example, it's common to see *have* written as *haue* and *use* as *vse*.

The letter *w* has an interesting relationship to the *u* and the *v*. It also was a late addition to the Latin alphabet. In printed form it is made by joining two *v's*, but in manuscript it usually appears as two *u's*. The French named it *doublevay*, or "double vee." French, of course, is more obliged to Latin than is the Germanic-oriented English language, in which the letter is called "double u." The Germans call it "way" and almost invariably give it the sound of *v*, which is why *Wagner* is "Vagner" and why many English-speaking Germans say "vot," "vy," and "ven."

As a further token of the trinity of *u-v-w*, it's interesting that they appear in just that order in the English alphabet. Interesting, too, that there are no *w*-words in the Latin-blooded Italian and Spanish vocabularies. And that in French, *u* always takes the *w*-sound when followed by a vowel, which is why *Louise* is "Luweeze" and *oui, oui* is "wee, wee."

The word-student soon adjusts to the *manuscript u*. He readily reads *beneuolens* as *benevolens* and *uolumen* as *volumen*, for example. He also reads *uirigo* as *virigo*, which brings up an interesting thought:

Virigo means virgin. It is a compound of *vir*, man + *igo*, less. But *virgin*, "manless," obviously is a misnomer when applied to males, as it frequently is. By imaginative extension, the equivalent word for the male would be something like "femigin," or "fegin," from a hypothetical *feminigo, femigo,* meaning "*woman*less." Why is there no such word? Because those who wear the pants regard virginity as a feminine strength but a masculine weakness, and seek no such *vnuirile* labels.

'with'

(if you were with it,
you were against it)

With is a turnabout word, a word which has completely reversed an earlier meaning. It began as the short form of the Old English *wither,* "against," which derived from the Germanic *wi'th,* also "against."

This ancient meaning is preserved in such present-day words as *withhold,* "hold against or from," and *withstand,* "stand against." Also in such expressions as "argue with," "do battle with," "at odds with," etc. *With* is seen in numerous Old English compounds, e.g., *withfeohtan,* "to fight against."

The word *withsay* is obsolete, but in meaning it was identical with that other archaism, *gainsay,* which is still seen occasionally. "I cannot gainsay you" means "I cannot say against you." Note that *contra-dict* also means "say against."

During that period when *with* meant "against," the word *mid* was used to mean "with." As in *amid.* Also as in *midwife,* "withwoman," i.e., the *woman with* the mother. Note the kinship of *mid* to the modern German *mit,* meaning "with."

'pig'

(Tom's was no squealer)

o.o.o.

When you encounter o.o.o. in an etymological dictionary, don't expect to learn much about the word you're interested in. It means "of obscure origin."

There are several *pigs* in the English language, and the one meaning "young porker" is o.o.o. Its Middle English form was *pigge,* a cognate of the Middle Dutch *pigge* which has become the modern Dutch *bigge* and *big,* and that's about all we know.

Some of the other *pigs* are much more interesting.

There's *pig,* the smelting term, meaning an ingot of metal, as in pig-iron. When ironworkers tapped the furnace, the molten metal ran through a main channel into a large mold. From this large mold, smaller streams ran to smaller molds. This reminded the ironworkers of a brood of pigs suckling their dam, so they called the ingot from the large mold "sow" and the smaller ingots "pigs."

Then, unfortunately, there's "pig," a contemptuous slang term for *girl.* It would be unfair to blame this barbarism on the Danes, whose legitimate word for girl is *pige,* but the coincidence is worth remarking. (If blame is to be placed, best evidence is that this *pig* originated in Canada in the the 1930s.)

But most surprising of all is the *pig* in the nursery rhyme:

> *Tom, Tom, the Piper's son,*
> *stole a pig and away he run;*
> *The pig was eat*
> *and Tom was beat*
> *and Tom went howling down*
> *the street.*

Despite all the kiddie-book drawings of Tom fleeing with a squealing porker under his arm — despite, indeed, what we've been told at our mothers' knees — Tom's pig wasn't a real pig. It was a pie baked in the shape of a pig. Such "pigs" were hawked on the streets by pie-men, as in that other nursery rhyme, "Simple Simon met a pie-man." Tom simply snatched his pig-pie and ran. This revelation, to be confirmed by *Oxford Dictionary of Nursery Rhymes,** brings Tom back to the status of ordinary boy and proves that truth is sometimes less strange than fiction.

*Not to be confused with *The Oxford Nursey Rhyme Book.*

'rape'

(Tom was guilty)

The word *rape* is so notorious for its best-known meaning that it gets little credit for its other meanings:

It is the name of a plant of the mustard family.

Also the name of an English county division.

Also the name for what's left after the juice is taken from grapes.

At one time it was a verb meaning to hasten. In *Piers Plowman* (1377) there is the line, "Awake. . .and rape thee to shrift," meaning "Get up, and hurry to confession."

And what a blow, on looking into Pope's *The Rape of the Lock,* to discover that the rape was nothing more than the petty theft of a lock of hair from a lady known as Belinda!

Theft, of course, is the overriding meaning behind the *rape* that makes headlines. Not stealthy, sneak-theft, but overt, brazen, violent theft. That's the sense born with the word, from the Latin *rapere,* to take by force, to seize and carry off.

Within this sense, *rape* had still another meaning. It meant to seize food, steal it, grab it and wolf it down. Tom, the Piper's Son, was a rapist when he grabbed that "pig" and crammed it into his mouth, in flight. (See *'pig',* preceding).

The word *ravine* is from the same Latin root that gave us *rape.* A ravine is the handiwork of erosion, the seizing and carrying away of soil by torrents and trickles.

Similarly, there is the *raven.* Internationally famous for stealing food, and perpetually hungry. Ravenous, you might say.

'nickname'

(also, *riding* and *anatomy* lessons)

There are more five-year-olds who know what a nickname is than there are fifty-year-olds who know why it's called *nick*name.

The *nick-* begins with the Old English verb *ecan* and its derivant *eke,* meaning to add to, to supplement. One who "ekes out a living" supplements his regular income with side jobs. Similarly, an *eke*name was a name supplementing a regular name, or in addition to it. The word was pronounced with an unstressed *e,* "ickname."

Question: How did an *ick*name become a *nick*name?

Answer: Exactly as that question demonstrates. The *n* deserted the article *an,* and moved over to become the first letter, or sound, in the noun.

Here we encounter two very significant language characteristics, *coalescence* and *metanalysis.*

Coalescence is the running together of sounds.

Metanalysis, a term coined by the great linguist, Otto Jespersen, is the reseparation of those sounds into words which are quite different from the originals.

Ewt, for example, was the original form of *newt,* just as was *ick*name of *nick*name. The sounds of the two words *an ewt* coalesced, and by metanalysis subsequently were reseparated into *a newt.* The same thing happened to convert *nurchin, nauger, napron* and *nadder* into *urchin, auger, apron* and *adder.*

Or consider the Yorkshire term *riding,* which designates any one of that county's three divisions, North Riding, East Riding, and West Riding. Certainly the term *riding* in this usage must be bewildering to many who know its meaning but not its reason for meaning what it means. Left to their own devices to explain it, they probably would associate it with the only other "riding" they know, assume that it refers to that part of land over which a man on horseback might ride in a specified period of time, and thus fall into folk etymology's trap. *Riding* here is a result of coalescence and metanalysis. The Old Saxon *thriding* meant "thirding," thus a third part or one of three divisions. But the sounds of *East Thriding, West Thriding,* and *North Thriding,* just naturally invited coalescence. Especially *North Thriding,* which came out as one word, "Northriding," and then by metanalysis was re-separated, i.e., "North *Riding.*"

Coalescence has opened the way for some interesting bits of false etymology.

It once was believed, for example, that *anatomy* was a coalescence of *an atomy.* For this reason, *anatomy* was sometimes "re-separated" into *a natomy.* This illogic was supported by the fact that the Greek *tome* means "a cutting," as in appende*ctomy,* tonsille*ctomy,* etc.

47

And as in the word *atom*, which as *a-tom* means *un*-cuttable, hence indivisible. When Shakespeare's Mistress Quickly raged, "Thou *atomy*, thou!" she was using the term as a synonym for "skinny," i.e., uncuttable, no flesh to cut, nothing but bones.

Actually, *anatomy* is neither *an atomy* or *a natomy*. It has no relationship whatever to *a* or *an*. It derives, quite simply, from the Greek *anatemnein,* meaning "to cut up." An uf of this.

′i—j—y′

(trinity is unity)

In Italian, the personal pronoun "I" is *io*.

In French it is *je*.
In Spanish it is *yo*.

The Latin *Iesu*,
English *Jesus*,
is pronounced *'Yay-su'.*

The Scottish 'John' =*Ian*.
The Dutch is *Jan*.
Both are pronounced *'Yahn.'*

The Breton *ia*
and Lithuanian *je*
are the English *yes*

and the Latin *iuuvenis*
(English *juvenile)*
has the Sanskrit equivalent *yuva. . .*

. . .while the English 'Jew' is the Greek *Ioudaios*,
German *Jude*,
and Hebrew *Yehudhi.*

Here thirteen different languages are involved in just a few examples of what might be called 'the i — j — y trinity' — a *unity*, really, in which the sounds represented by these letters stand in for each other in uncountable instances and in most or all

Indo-European languages.

The *i* is called *iota* in Greek and Latin and *yodh* in Hebrew. As the smallest letter of the Greek alphabet, it gave the name *iota* word-status by making it stand for smallness. Smallness to the point of insignificance, as in the expression "not one iota." Or as in the King James Bible dictum, "one *jot* or one tittle shall in no wise pass from the law, till all be fulfilled" *(Matthew: 5:18)*. The word *jot* is a transliteration of *iota,* another example of the *i — j* kinship.

The *i* wasn't dotted until about the 11th century. The dot was added to solve a problem, to keep the *i* from being read as a part of the letter adjacent to it. An undotted *i* for example, frequently made a preceding *n* look like an *m*. And two together, as in *filii,* were easily misread as *u*.

This is the very problem to which the *j* owes its existence. While some scribes dotted the *i* to separate it from adjacent letters, others wrote it in a "prolonged" form, letting it descend below the line. In time, handwriting curved its lower extremity into the tail of the modern *j,* and somewhat simultaneously, it inherited the dot.

It wasn't until the 17th century that the *j* was established as an independent letter of the English alphabet — the King James Bible, when published in 1611, was known as the King *Iames* — and even then its popular use as "another i" continued for more than a hundred years.

The kinship of *j* to *y* is seen in many languages. The English *jerk,* once written *yerk,* is typical. The bird-name spelled *jaeger* is pronounced "yager." The German *jung* is the English *young,* and Yonkers, N.Y., owes its name to the Dutch *jonker,* "squire," who once lived there.

The kinship of *y* and *i* is much greater. We see it when *day* becomes *daily* and when *money* turns into *monies*. Also when words such as *carry, marry* and *tarry* become *carried, married* and *tarried*. "Holy-ness" is *holiness* and "happyness" is *happiness*. In some cases, we see the *i* substituting for *y,* as in *smith* for the earlier *smyth, his* for *hys,* etc. In other cases, *y* has replaced *i,* as in the Old English *nimphe,* modern English *nymph*. And in *gymnasium,* we use *y* for the vowel-sound *i* and *i* for the consonant-sound *y*.

Keep this *i — j — y* trinity in mind. It'll help to clarify some of the word stories that follow, by yymyni.

'Jew'

(it once stood for 'Southerner')

A Virginia writer referred to "a New Jersey Jewish accent" and a reader promptly challenged her to explain the difference between that and a Virginia Jewish accent.

That's easy.

New Jersey Jews say "youse" and Virginia Jews say "you-all."

Of course, the same facetious thing can be said of Jersey and Virginia Catholics, Lutherans, Buddhists or atheists — the point being that "Jewish" describes a religious belief, not an accent, a language, or a nationality. Sammy Davis, Jr.'s accent is every bit as "Jewish" as Molly Goldberg's, because neither is "Jewish."

The term *Jew* derives ultimately from the name of the Hebrew patriarch Yehudha ("The Praised"), which is represented in contemporary English Bibles as *Judah.*

The Hebrew equivalent of *Jew,* as represented by the English alphabet, is *yehudi,* pronounced *y'udi.* The Latin form, *Iudaeus* (pronounced "Yudaeus," see *'i — j — y'* preceding) was the immediate origin of the French *Juif,* Spanish *Judio,* English *Jew* and German *Jude.* The Italians prefer *ebreo* and *ebrea,* masculine and feminine forms meaning "Hebrew."

Middle English spellings of the name varied from *giu* and *gyu* to *iu, iuw,* and *iuwe.* Shakespeare's indecision is typified in the line, "I am a Iewe; Hath not a Iew eyes?"

Although Judaism is a religion, not a place, the term *Jew* is not altogether free of geographical significance. It was scarcely used until after Judah's southern kingdom of Israel had survived the northern kingdom in the 7th century B.C. Today it designates any adherent of Judaism, but there was a time when it simply distinguished a southern Israelite from his northern brother.

'Yiddish'

(it's more -*dish* than *Yid*-)

Many people think of Yiddish as "some sort of Jewish accent" and are surprised to know that it's a mature, legitimate language spoken by an estimated 5 to 10 million Jews, of whom several millions live on this side of the Atlantic.

Yiddish is fundamentally a German tongue. (The name itself is a corruption of the German term *Jude-Deutsch,* or "Jew-German," influenced somewhat by the German adjective *Judisch,* or "Jewish"). It became an independent language when the Ashkenazic Jews, driven from their Middle Rhine homes during the Crusades, settled in scattered groups from the Baltic to the Black Seas. By the 18th century it was the language of practically all Eastern European Jews, retaining the German dialect although written in the Hebrew alphabet. It has been estimated that its vocabulary today is about 70% German, 10% Balto-Slavic, and 20% Hebrew and the related Aramaic. In this light, Yiddish, or Jude-Deutsch, is considerably more -*dish* than *Yid*-.

Hitler murdered some 6 million Yiddish-speaking Jews, and in 1948 the Israeli government declared Hebrew to be the official language of the new nation. It's possible that these two actions have spelled the doom of Yiddish. Let's hope not; it is uniquely warm, colorful, and human, and it has made some refreshing contributions to our own language. Run your eye down the following list – you may be surprised to see that some of our typical Americanisms are typical Yiddishisms:

bubu – a little blunder, a minor "goof"
mazuma – from *mezumen,* "ready cash"
phooey – *fooy,* reinforced by German *pfui,* "for shame!"
gezuntheit – "good health", "bless you"
slob – from *szhlob, zhlob,* "moron"
shush – Yiddish "hush!"
schnook – a dumbbell, a sucker
schmaltz – sweet-talk; corny flattery
kindergarten – kindergarten, "kindergarden"
strudel – Yiddish *shtrudel*
kibitzer – meddlesome on-looker
borsht – beet (or cabbage) soup

Oi, Oy — Yiddish *Oh,* to express surprise, pain, rapture or disgust

shvitser — blow-hard, braggart

gelt — money

goniff, ganef — thief, robber

schlock — from Yiddish shlak, "cut-rate, junky"

chutzpeh — cheek, gall

meshugener — "a crazy nut"

'*Ladino*'

(the Spanish Yiddish)

Ladino is the Romance-language counterpart of the Germanic Yiddish. It is the mother-tongue of about 150,000 Sephardic Jews, most of whom now live in Greece, Turkey, and Bulgaria, where their ancestors settled after their expulsion from Spain in 1496-1501. An estimated 20,000 Israeli speak Ladino.

The language is every bit as Spanish as Yiddish is German, with words added from the Greek, Hebrew, and Turkish tongues. (Don't confuse *Ladino* with *Ladin,* which is another name for that Rhetian tongue spoken in southeastern Switzerland).

'*drawing room*'

(and *boudoir,* where long faces were drawn)

A drawing room is a *with*drawing room from which the *with* has been dropped.

It was the room to which the women *withdrew* when the hostess said, "And now, ladies, shall we leave the gentlemen to their cigars?"

The more affluent ladies of that bygone day had still another withdrawing room. A private one, to which they might withdraw and pout to their heart's content. It was called *boudoir,* from the French *bouder,* meaning "to pout."

The lord of the manor also had a private pouting sanctum. At first, it too was called *boudoir.* But the little lady changed all that.

If there was pouting to do, she'd do it. After that, when she went
to her boudoir, her husband went to his den, the beast.

'etc.'

(a pleonasm we can forgive)

Etc., abbreviation of the Latin *et cetera*, also written *et caetera*,
is a loyal friend of man. It relieves us of a great deal of
responsibility, makes us appear more fully informed than we are,
comes in handy as a way of ending sentences, and is loved and
understood by all who use it.

Understood *generally*, that is to say. As for a precise
understanding — well, how about you? Here are five definitions of
et cetera and *et caetera*, picked from assorted dictionaries. All are
correct for all practical purposes, but only one is a correct literal
translation. See if you can spot it:

> "and so forth"
> "and the like"
> "and so on"
> "and and others"
> "and the rest."

If you aren't sure, here's a clue: *Caetera*, the earlier form of
cetera, is a compound of two Indo-European words, *cae*, meaning
"and," and *etero*, meaning "other."

Caetera and *cetera*, then, historically and traditionally, mean
"and others." When *et* is added, the literal translation becomes
"*and* and others." This, of course, is a pleonasm we can forgive
easier than amend.

Here are three other very common Latin abbreviations worth a
little refresher course. Refresh yourself by lining up the
abbreviation at left with its correct meaning at right:

> *i.e.* —————"to wit"
> *e.g.* —————"for example"
> *viz.* —————"that is to say"

By transposing *i.e.* and *viz.*, above, you'll have the correct line-up: *i.e.* stands for *id est*, "that is to say"; *e.g.* for *exempli grata*, "for (free) example," and *viz.* is an abbreviation of *videlicet*, itself a coalescence of *videre licet*, meaning "it is permissible to see," "to witness," "to wit," etc., etc., etc.

****

Here are a few more Latin abbreviations constantly encountered by people who read books like this, perhaps worth passing in review:

ab. init.	ab initio	from the beginning
ad init.	ad initio	to the beginning
ad fin	ad finem	to the end
ad int.	ad interim	meanwhile
ad lib	ad libitum	at one's pleasure
ad loc.	ad locum	to or at the place
aet.	aetatis	at the age of
a.h.l.	ad hunc locum	at this place
brev.	brevarium	abridgement
c., ca.	circa	about (the time of)
cf.	confer	compare
crast.	crastinus	tomorrow, later
d.s.p.	decessit sine prole	died without issue
D.V.	Deo volente	God willing
e.o.	ex officio	no longer in office
et al	et alibi	and elsewhere
et alii*		and others*
et seq.	et sequens	and following
ined.	ineditus	not published
mat.	matutinum	morning
ms.	manuscript	manuscript

*This Latin "and others" is in no wise in contradiction of *et cetera*, "and others." *Caetera* is a borrowing from the Greek, in which can be seen the *etero* of *hetero-*, meaning "other," as in *heterosexual love*, i.e., love of the *other* sex. The "purer Latin" *alii* has the same root that gives *alternate, alter ego*, etc.

mss.	manuscripts	manuscripts
n.b.	nota bene	note well, pay attention
nol. con.	nole contendere	I do not wish to argue
non seq.	non sequitur	it does not follow
q.v.	quod vide	which see ("look it up")
sc.	scilicet	namely
s.f.	sub finem	near the end
ut dict.	ut dictum	as ordered

'bullish' and 'bearish'

(and how to keep them straight)

The word *bull* (bovine, not papal or literary) apparently started with the Indo-European *bhel,* meaning "to swell." Yes, alas, in a phallic sense; facts when embarrassing are facts still.

The Old English form was *bula.* It was related to the Old Norse *boli* and Middle Low German *bulle,* and also to the Swedish *bulin,* meaning "swollen." *Bula* narrowed to the Middle English *bule,* which subsequently lost its *e* and became the modern *bull.*

A *bullish* stock market, therefore, is one that is swelling, rising, virile.

Its opposite, *bearish,* has an origin that's more presentable in mixed company. It derives from an old fable in which a hunter comes to regret having sold a bearskin before he killed the bear, and from the resultant English proverb, "Don't sell the skin until you've shot the bear." In London's Exchange Alley, this admonition referred to the practice of brokers who sold a stock for future delivery, expecting its price to go down before they had to buy. The name for this kind of operater was "bearskin jobber."

To keep *bullish* and *bearish* straight, just think of one as Freudian and the other as Fraudian.

'kiss'

(and why *xxx* means *kiss kiss kiss*)

"Lord, I wonder what fool it was that first invented kissing," said Jonathan Swift, and it makes you think.

Kissing, it seems, was indeed an invention. There's a great deal of scientific if prudish evidence that the kiss, at first, was only a simple salutation. No more erotic meaning than a handshake, until man began to see what he had got hold of.

Today the word *kiss* is both a noun and a verb. But this hasn't always been so. The early Old English noun was *coss.* The verb was *cyssan,* which in Middle English became *kysse* and *kisse.* To kisse somebody was to give him a coss. This explains the Wyclif Bible translation, "And he cam to Jhesu to *kisse* him; an Jhesu seide to him, Judas, with a *coss* thou betrayest mannys sone."

In medieval times, signers of wills, deeds and other documents always added an *x* after their signatures. If they couldn't write, as was frequently the case, they still used the *x.* It was regarded as the St. Andrew's Cross (not the Calvary Cross, use of which was considered irreverent), and symbolized the putting of the hand on the Bible while taking an oath.

It was the custom to kiss the *x*, after marking it on a document, to symbolize the kissing of the Bible. In time, *x* came to stand for any kind of a kiss, and went on to become one of the world's leading mail-order products.

(The *X* in *Xmas,* incidentally, is not quite as irreverent as it seems. Not quite. It is the Greek letter *x,* which is pronounced *chi* and which, as every Sigma Chi knows, is equivalent to the English digraph *ch.* The X in *Xmas,* therefore, is an abbreviation of *Christ,* somewhat like writing *Cmas.* Anybody so busy he has to write *Xmas* for Christmas is too busy).

Some scholars see kissing as a dangerous game. More than 40,000 microbes live on one square centimeter of human lip. But nothing is all bad. One thing about kissing, it keeps people off the streets.

'island'

(a little learning is a dangerous thing)

When you were a tyke, full of round-eyed trust, the teacher told you that *i-s* spells *is*. But the first time you came to grips with the word *island,* she shook her head. "Not *is*-land," she said, "*i*-land." And no amount of reasoning, that if *island* is called *iland* it should be spelled *iland,* would move her.

But there's a moral victory, better late than never, in the fact that once upon a time, she'd have had to agree with you. In the English of some 500 years ago, *island* was, indeed, spelled *iland.*

But then — came the *Renaissance.*

There's no doubt that the Renaissance, or Revival of Learning, as it's sometimes called, was beneficial to the English language in many ways (see *Foreword*). But it's a good wind that blows no ill. It also provided the limelight which pedantry seeks like a moth and the stage on which it was proven, as Pope later observed, that a little learning is a dangerous thing. Along with its competent and dedicated scholars, the Revival of Learning was infiltrated by intellectual snobs and powerful phonies whose zest for learning was a poor, pale thing compared with their zest for exhibitionism and the having of their way.

As a result, many misdemeanors and felonies were committed in the name of improving the language. These slings and arrows of outrageous etymology seem trivial today, because we've learned to live with them as we have with the *s* in *island.* But it takes only a little imagination to see what a bucking and rearing there'd be if someone came along today to force similar "improvements" down our English-speaking throats:

Drunk on the Greek and Latin classics, these pseudo-intellectuals decided that the English word *iland* should have an *s* because the French word *isle* has one. There was no etymological basis for it. The French *isle* derives from the Latin *insula,* and the *s* is a part of its heritage. But *iland* was a Germanic word, with such early spellings as *iegland* and *eiland* (*ieg* from a varying Indo-European root typified by *eku,* aqua, water) and never an *s* to its name.

These were the men who delved into Latin for the *b* they put in *doubt, debt* and *subtle.*

Comptroller is their re-spelling of *controller,* arrived at by a mis-association with the French *compt,* count.

They turned *vittles* into *victuals, receit* into *receipt,* and *indit* into *indict,* although the pronunciations have remained the same.

Having decided, wrongly, that *sissors* derived from the Latin *scindere,* "to cleave," they converted it to *scissors—* and by the same false etymology, transformed *sythe* to *scythe.*

Coud was the past tense of *can.* It had no relationship whatever to *should* and *would.* But *should* and *would* had an *l,* and so *coud* became *could.*

Latin-sprung words were remodeled to admit Greek classical blood – of the wrong type. The Greek *anchorite,* "hermit," was spelled with an *h,* and so the Old English *ancor,* from Latin *ancora,* received the transfusion that gives us *anchor.* And although the name *Antony* had gotten along without criticism since long before Cleopatra breathed "Antonius" into Marc's ear, the classics-combers needed only a peek at the Greek *anthos,* meaning "flower," to convert it to *Anthony.*

Artur, Caterine and *Dorothy* became *Arthur, Catherine* and *Dorothy. Esther* is still pronounced as when it was *Ester,* and *Thames* is still "Temmes", but the pronunciation changed along with the spelling when *trone* became *throne* and *autor* became *author.*

But time heals everything, and we shouldn't be too hard on these early bulls in the English word shop. Perhaps it's something in the national blood. How else can we explain a nation that calls a derby a *darby* and a lieutenant a *leftenant*? And if we can't explain *that,* how will we ever explain one that spells Arkansaw *Arkansas?*

'landscape'

(and why Englishmen say "shedule")

The word *landscape* is a souvenir of the Old English period, when the sound of *sh* was written as *sc.* "Ship" and "shall" for example, were spelled *scip* and *scal.* "Fish" was *fisc* and "wash" was *wascan.* Similarly, "landshape" was spelled *landscape.*

The re-spelling of *sc* as *sh* is the work of the Norman scribes who followed William the Conqueror into England. The Latin and Norman French languages to which they were accustomed had no well-defined digraph to represent the English *sh*-sound, especially as the beginning of a word. Accordingly, they tried various alphabetical forms, including *s, ss, sch* and *sh,* the latter winning out and still prevailing.

In some cases, the re-spelled word pushed its predecessor into oblivion. *Sceap* (sheep), for instance, and *biscop* (bishop), as well as *scip, scal, fisc,* and *wascan,* just mentioned.

But in others, the old form survived along with the new, usually with a closely related meaning:

scale and *shale*

scour and *shower*

sk(c)irt and *shirt*

scuffle and *shuffle*

scallion and *shallot*

scabby and *shabby*

scatter and *shatter*

scepter and *shaft (from "shefter")*

In Old English, *scholar* was written *scoler* and pronounced "sholer." It wasn't until the Revival of Learning (see *Foreword*) that Classics-minded Englishmen returned to the word's Latin ancestor, *scholaris,* for the presentday *scholar.*

Englishmen today pronounce *schedule* as "shedule." Americans prefer "skedule." It is tempting but false etymology to attribute the English pronunciation to the old *sc = sh* phonology. It results instead from *schedule*'s late Middle English form, *sedule,* "sedjul," a derivation of the Old French *cedule.* Here again, the

Renaissancists turned to the Classics, to the early Latin *scedula* which, thanks to the influence of the transliterated Greek *chi,* was by medieval times spelled *schedula.* But despite the Renaissance re-spelling, *schedule,* Englishmen continued with the old pronunciation, "sedjul," until about 1800 — at which time they began to recognize the *sch* as *sh,* hence "shedule."

In the U.S., Noah Webster insisted that since *ch* is not a Latin symbol, in *schedule* it obviously is a transliteration of the Greek *chi,* with the *k*-sound as in *chorus,* and that *schedule* therefore must be pronounced "skedule."

Who is right, the Americans or the English?

The Americans, of course. Unless — as Noah Webster pointed out — the English have enough faith in themselves to pronounce *scheme* as "sheme" and *schism* as "shism." Noah Webster was a hard man to beat. He was a good pronouncer.

Back to *landscape.* It is somewhat a maverick. Instead of respelling it land*shape* to fit the Old English pronunciation, we have repronounced it land*scape* to fit the Old English spelling. A scameful inconsistency.

'aloof'

(starboard has nothing to do with the stars)

On ancient ships, the steering-oar was always located on the right side. The Old English word for this side was *steorbord,* a compound of *steor,* "steer" + *bord,* "side" (as in *border).* Thus *starboard,* as *steorbord* came to be called, is the right side of the vessel.

The left side was called *ladebord,* the side on which the vessel was laded, or loaded, to keep the steering-oar in the clear.

Ladebord assimilated into *larbord* (its *d*-sound took the stronger *r*-sound; see *'stark-naked').* But *larbord* sounded too much like *starboard.* Shouted directions were too easily misunderstood by the helmsman. *Larbord* was dropped and *port,* also a reference to the loading side, the "port-side," took its place.

The name of the steering-oar was *lof.* The command, "Hard alof!" (or *a-luff)* meant "Hard on the oar!", i.e., *steer away from.* The Middle English pronunciation of *lof* was *loof,* hence the present-day *aloof,* to describe someone who avoids or "steers away" from others.

'lust'

(ships listed to starboard
before sailors lusted in port)

Many of our words suggesting strength begin with the same letters *strength* begins with — *stamina, sturdy, stalwart, staunch, steadfast, stocky, stout, stud, stable, stanchion, standard, stallion,* etc.

Similarly, the letter *l* seems to lead as a starter for a certain class of sex-words, e.g., *lust, libido, lecher, lascivious, lewd, licentious, libertine,* etc.

Like so many of our other somewhat hush-hush words, these "l"-words had quite innocent beginnings.

Lewd once meant nothing worse than "common," and probably is kin to *layman.*

Lecher meant only "glutton"; the first lecher chased nothing spicier than food.

Libido, libidinous, derive from the Latin *libet,* which meant "it pleases" and was suggestive to only the most suggestable minds.

Licentious originally meant one who permits generously — and *generally.* Today it means one who permits generously — and *specifically.*

Libertine at first meant a freedman, later a free thinker, and finally one who is free of all moral restraint.

Lascivious, in its youth, meant nothing worse than inclining or leaning. Or *listing,* as a ship does. This is doubly noteworthy, because *lust* at first was a variant form of *list* — a relationship that is better understood when we consider how *listless* describes a *lustless* man. Or woman.

'root'

(as of garlic, radishes, and words)

The Indo-European verb *ra* meant "to grow from, to derive from."

It went into the Greek as *ram* and *rhad,* and into the Latin and Germanic as *rad.*

In the Germanic, *rad* had a variant form, *rot,* which was a development of the sound-shifts explained in the *Foreword.*

This variant form, *rot,* went through the Old Norse and Old Frisian and into Old English without a change. It was pronounced "root," just as the Old English pronunciation of *Domesday* and *Rome* were "Doomsday" and "Room." At some time during the Middle English period it was re-spelled *roote,* and later the terminal *e* characteristic of that period was dropped, leaving the present-day *root.*

Meanwhile, the Latin *rad* had produced assorted kindred words. One of them led to the Italian *radice,* which became the French *radis,* which itself became the English *radish,* which, of course, is a root. The Latin language also borrowed the Greek *ram* to produce *ramus,* "branch," from which comes the verb *ramify,* to branch out. *Ramus* also is an ancestor of the Old English *hrameson,* Middle English *ramson* or *ramsin,* an archaic name for wild garlic. Which also is a root.

Let's hope that all this rooting around with *root* will summon forth all your root-consciousness, linguistically speaking. This book frequently refers to the Indo-European and Germanic roots which are the foundations of words it treats, and this is a good time to ask you to note:

As the *Foreword* explains, Indo-European and Germanic are hypothetical languages. Traditionally, words from hypothetical languages are preceded by an asterisk to indicate that they are arrived at by educated speculation, not by written records. For example, the Indo-European root of the modern word *gusto* would be designated as "IE *geus.*" This book will depart the tradition, forego the asterisk, and ask you to bear in mind that any word labeled Indo-European or Germanic is a hypothetical word.

About 2,000 Indo-European roots have been established with some degree of certainty. The following is a representative sample, in which the roots' similarities to their English descendants are easily seen:

Root	Meaning	English
su	"bear, bring forth"	son
poi	"to drink"	potion
op	"work"	operate
reidh	"to go"	ride, road
semi	"half"	semi-
ost	"bone"	ossify
poti	"lord"	potentate
do	"to give"	donate
mori	"sea"	marine
pa	"to nurture"	pastor
kan	"to sing"	cant, chant
me-not	"month, moon"	menstruate
kap	"to seize"	capture
enomn	"name"	nominate
rod	"to scratch"	rodent
kes	"to cut"	castrate
bhendh	"bind"	bundle
lou	"to wash"	lotion
ger	"to grow older"	geriatrics
dei	"bright, to shine"	deity
gherdu	"to enclose"	gird, garden
wer	"to speak"	word, verb
sna, na	"to flow"	nautical, nurse
gwena	"woman"	gynecology
trei	"three"	tri-, ter-
kered	"heart"	cardiac
pak	"to make fast"	pact
ped	"foot"	pedal
spek	"to look"	spectator
ker	"horn"	cornet
meg (h)	"big"	magnify
wedi	"to see"	video
der	"to run"	dromedary
gen	"to beget"	generation
pet, pt	"to fly"	pterodactyl
mus	"mouse"	muscle
bak	"rod, staff"	bacteria
plak	"wide, flat"	fluke

deru, dru	"tree"	tree
del	"to count"	teller
k(h)ar	"hard"	hard

In *pet, pt,* "to fly," you see the origin of the *pt* in *helicopter.** The root *mus,* "mouse", became *muscle,* thanks to the Greeks; to them the ripple of a muscle under the skin was like a mouse scurrying along under a cloth, and they nicknamed it just that, "mouse," or *mus. Bacteria,* of course, relates to *bak* because bacteria are rod-shaped.

In the last four roots and derivations listed above, there are three examples of the Germanic shift away from certain Indo-European consonant sounds: *plak/fluke,* the shift from *p* to *f; deru/tree* and *del/teller,* the shift from *d* to *t,* and *kar/hard,* the shift from *k* to *h.* That makes this a good place to —

HALT!

At the beginning of this book, there is that preliminary known as the *Foreword,* or *Preface.*

Did you skip the preliminary?

If so, why not turn back and take it in? As you've just seen, in this book there will be references to consonant-shifts and other linguistic phenomena which, until known, camouflage the relationships of many related words. They're easily understood and simply explained. Besides, you *paid* for the Foreword. If you skip it, you've spent wastefully. Wasteful spending feeds inflation. The way things are now, if you skip the Foreword, who knows, you might bankrupt us all.

**Helico,* from the Greek *heliko,* means a spiral, a turning, a roll, and refers to the helicopter's rotor blades.

'colloquialism'

(something many college professors don't know)

To hear a boy say he "carried" his girl to a party is to wonder whether the young lady was crippled or just lazy.

Except in certain parts of the South, where to *carry* a girl somewhere is simply to *take* her there. If this seems odd, hold on — is it any odder, when you think about it, than *taking* her there?

Three out of four college graduates, including quite a few professors, will identify this expression as a *colloquialism.* They'll be wrong. It's a *provincialism.* A provincialism, as any good dictionary will show, is quite different from a colloquialism.

A colloquialism is a laxly, informally-pronounced word, as opposed to the precise and proper way of expressing the same word. Colloquialisms are conveniences to the tongue, perpetuated in writing. *Can't,* for example, is a colloquialism, a convenient way of saying *can not.* So is *o'clock,* for the long-dead *of clock.* Sometimes a colloquialism can be several words pronounced as one — *shouldn't've,* for instance, for *should not have.*

On the other hand, a provincialism is a word or phrase spoken in a manner peculiar to a certain *province,* or locality. This identification with *location* may contribute to the confusion of *provincialism* with *colloquialism.* The Latin root of *location* is *locus,* which closely resembles *loqui,* the Latin root of *colloquialism* (seen also in *eloquent, loquacious*).

But the big reason for the mix-up lies in the fact that many colloquialisms are colloquialisms *of* provincialisms. "Y'all" is a colloquialism of the provincialism "You-all." Just as "youse" sometimes is a colloquial form of the colloquialism "you'uns" *(you-ones).*

Some girls are *taken* to parties and *carried* home.

'film'

(and why our fathers are not our pathers)

Photographic film gets its name from the thin skin, or film, of light-sensitive chemicals that covers one side of it.

But why is this thin film itself called *film?*

Shakespeare offers a clue in *As You Like It:* "We are still handling our ewes," says one of the shepherds, "and their *fels,* you know, are greasie'"

Fel was an Old English word meaning skin, or hide. Also spelled *fell,* as in the obsolete *thrutsfell,* leprosy, and *fellmonger,* hide-seller, this word derived from the Germanic *fello, fellam.* It was closely related to the Old Frisian *fel,* Gothic *fill,* and the modern German and Icelandic *fell,* all meaning skin or hide.

Another derivative of *fello, fellam,* was the Old English *filmen.* Like *fel,* it meant skin, but more specifically a very thin skin, a membrane, as in *aegfelma,* "egg-skin." This *filmen* became the Middle English *filme,* modern English *film.*

Here we have a fine example of the sound-shift described in the *Foreword.* In the Indo-European mother tongue, the word for skin was *pello,* or *pellam.* Whereas the Greek and Latin daughter-tongues retained the phonetic *p* in *pella* and *pellis* (whence such present-day words as *pelt* and *pellagra*), their Germanic sister-tongue converted it to *f,* for *fello, fellam.*

If it weren't for this sound shift, here in the U.S. we'd curse plat tires instead of flat tires, go pishing instead of fishing, wear pelt hats instead of felt hats, pay pees instead of fees, and call our fathers Pather. And the film in our cameras would be, that's right, *pilm.*

'won't'

(where there's a will,
there once was a *wol*)

Most people look at *won't* as a contraction of *will not,* which is the wrong way to look at it.

Wol is the word that meant "will" before the word *will* meant "will," and *won't* is a contraction of *wol not,* i.e., *woln't.* To see how *woln't* became *won't,* just say it aloud several times.

This same process of colloquialism converted *shall not* to *shalln't* to *shan't.*

'wont'

(a verb and a noun born of an adjective)

"He was *wont* to drink a morning toddy."

"It was his *wont* to drink a morning toddy."

In the first of these sentences, the archaic *wont* is a verb; in the other, a noun. The relationship of the two is precisely that of their respective meanings:

"He was *accustomed* to a morning toddy."

"It was his *custom* to have a morning toddy."

Both derive from the Middle English adjective *wunt,* a narrowing of *woned,* which meant "accustomed." *Woned* was the past participle of the Old English *wunian,* to dwell (hence to remain with, to live with, to become accustomed to).

Toddy, usually whisky with hot, sweetened water, derives from the Hindu *tari,* the fermented juice of the palmyra tree. *Tari* becomes *toddy* by the cerebral pronunciation of *r,* the same thing that sometimes converts *terribly* to "teddibly."

'wean'

(to accustom or to disaccustom, that is the question)

The word *wean* is so closely related to *wont* (see preceding) that it's virtually the same word. Its Old English ancestor, *wenian,* was the Old English *wunian,* "to accustom," narrowed down to signify a single and specific kind of accustoming, that of the nursing babe to more solid foods. But since the female breast is more impressive than the utensils to which man ever afterward is doomed, *wean* in the popular mind has come to stand for *"dis*accustom" rather than "accustom."

The homonym, *ween,* means "suppose, suspect, imagine." It derives from the Middle English verb, *wenen.* "I know you better than you *wene,*" wrote Malory. "Nor turned, I *weene,* Adam from his Spouse," weened Milton.

'used to'

(a usage we are widely wont to use)

"I used to date him."

"This used to be the best part of town."

"I wear glasses now, but I didn't used to."

Used to is an odd figure of speech that doesn't seem odd until it's thought about. We grow up using it, seldom give it any thought.

Although etymologically unrelated to *wont* and *wean* (see preceding), its sense is the same, i.e., "accustomed." *To be accustomed or wont to do something, now only in past tense,* says the Oxford English Dictionary. Fowler also likens it to *wont:* "As an intransitive verb, meaning to be *wont* to, use is now confined to the past tense."

The English *use,* verb and noun, derives from the Latin *uti,* as do the equivalents, *utilize* and *utility.* The past participle of *uti* is *usus* (which probably is *utsus* with the *t* assimilated). *Usus* generated the Vulgar Latin verb *usare,* from which there proceeded the Old French noun and verb *us* and *user* and the Middle English *us* and *usen.* The Middle English forms later met in *use,* by which time a supplementary meaning had come along, "to follow a manner or course of life, to become accustomed to." The adverb *usually* delivers this same meaning, i.e., "customarily." The past tense, *used,* of course refers to a manner or course previously followed, an earlier custom, a former practice.

Used to has been used, or mis-used, at will. It is a grammatical Huck Finn, allowed to roam into such predicaments as "he didn't used to" and "he used not to," the latter a construction no less beautiful when the infinitive is split, "he used to not." Note that "he used not to" contorts colloquially into "He usedn't to."

None of this is to disparage *used to.* Like Huck himself, it has an untutored but earthy and unfeigned loveliness. Besides, it's quite useful. Without it, how would one express the difference between *he used used cars* and *he used to use used cars?*

'ye'

(a tale of a thorny twosome)

Once upon a time, this symbol:

$$þ$$

was a hard-working letter in the English alphabet. It should not be confused with the letter *p*, which it resembles. Its name was *thorn*, and the sound it represented was the one now represented by the digraph *th*, as in *thing, thin,* etc. Thus *þing* was pronounced "thing," *þ in* was pronounced "thin," and so on.

The thorn did not precede the digraph *th*. It just took its place for a while. Old texts show that it was used until about the end of the Middle English period, after which the digraph *th* was resurrected and standardized by printing.

Hereby hangs an interesting word tale:

Handwriting, by awkwardness or haste or both, often makes one letter look like another. An *o*, for example, frequently looks like an *a*, an *e* like an *l*, a *u* like a *v*, and so on. Thanks to faulty handwriting, the thorn, long before the advent of printing, had so often been written like this —

$$Y$$

— that it became confused with the letter *y*, to the extent that *y* in some instances was actually used to represent the *th*-sound.

One outstanding example of this is y^t , which with its small *t* was an abbreviation of *þat.* or *that.*

But the most memorable example is y^e . This abbreviated "the" was so common that it became a legitimate word, *ye,* flourishing for centuries as another form of the definite article, and seen even today in such pseudo-quaint usages as "Ye Olde Tea Shoppe."

Now to back-track a bit:

When the thorn came into use, the English alphabet already had a character to represent the *th*-sound. It was the Irish *d*, borrowed and crossed like a *t*, like this:

$$ð$$

— and although its correct name was *eth,* in time it was widely mis-labeled *thorn.* This is somewhat understandable, since it represented the same sound the thorn represented.

The question is, why were *two* characters used to represent the same sound?

The answer is, they weren't intended to represent the same sound. Technically, the eth expressed the voiced *th,* as in *then,* and the thorn stood for the voiceless *th,* as in *thick.** But nobody wanted to get that technical about it, so the two were used indiscriminately until ð finally disappeared during the Middle English period. It probably was for the best. One ðrn is sticky enough, but two þorns — ye gods.

'grog'

(or, *How Mount Vernon Got Its Name*)

In the British navy, during the time of George II, there was an admiral known as "Old Grog." For a good reason, but not the one the name suggests.

Raincoats hadn't been invented at the time, so the admiral invented one. He used a grogram coat (grogram being the cloth today's ladies know as *grosgrain*). To make it turn water, he soaked it in melted wax and gum, and it did the job just fine. But it was so stiff it would stand by itself, and the admiral make quite a spectacle when he wore it. Amused, his crews nicknamed him "Old Grog," for his grogram coat.

Now as you know, drinking is one of the crosses a poor seaman must bear, and at the time there was so much of it in His Majesty's navy that very few of His Majesty's seadogs were seaworthy. This was chronologically unfortunate, because the Spanish customs-house officials at Havana had just cut off Robert Jenkins'

---

*The terms *voiceless* and *voiced* are among the first encountered by the beginning student of linguistics. The words *thick* and *then,* above, demonstrate their meanings very nicely. Make the *th*-sound as in *thick.* You'll see that you don't need your voice — just a puff of air, the tongue and the teeth. This *th,* then, is *voiceless.* Now, make the same experiment with the *th* of *then.* You can hear and feel it come up from your vocal cords. This *th,* then, is *voiced.* For other examples, see "Consonant Shift," in the *Foreword.*

ear, and England and Spain were busily engaged in The War of Jenkins' Ear.

But Old Grog solved the problem. He cut the rum rations with water, half-and-half, on all the ships he commanded. It was such a good idea that it soon became Navy regulation. They even named the dilute potion for him, which is how the word *grog* came into the vocabulary.

Sailors being sailors, we might reasonably assume that this watering down of the booze would have made Old Grog a less than popular figure in the Navy — if, indeed, he hadn't disappeared over the side some dark night. But this wasn't the case. Old Grog was a man's man for a' that, and the men remained very fond of him.

One of them, an American colonial who was the half-brother of a boy who later made quite a name for himself in America, was so devoted to the admiral that when his hitch in the British Navy was up, he built a home for himself in Virginia and named it for his old commander, whose real name was Edward Vernon.

'phoney'

(thank Alexander Graham Bell for the spelling)

The Irish word for *ring*, the kind worn upon the finger, is *fainne*.

At one time in Ireland there were confidence men who lived by double-gilding cheap *fainnes* and planting them where they could be "found" while in the presence of some prosperous-looking innocent. The innocent, if he were innocent enough, usually wound up by buying the *fainne* for half of what it seemed to be worth and ten times what it was.

By the time this livelihood spread to England, the *fainne* was called "fawney." Con men who practiced it were known as fawney-droppers, fawney-bouncers, and just plain fawneys.

The word *fawney* migrated to the States with the Irish, but here the pronunciation was softened, and "phoney" became the name for fake jewelry, in vogue about 1920. A man who peddled fake jewelry was called a "phoney-man."

Why was the initial *f* converted to *ph*? Because of American ignorance of the word's original spelling and national consciousness of something that was just becoming a dramatic part of everyday life, the tele*phone.*

'shibboleth'

(why the Spanish won't call a spade a spade)

As Hebrews, the Ephraimites and the Gileadites spoke the same language, but with distinct dialectal differences. The Ephraimites, for example, were unable to handle words which started with the sound of *sh* – a fact which apparently was well known by the Gileadite sentries at the fords of the Jordan:

"Then they said unto him, Say now *Shibboleth;* and he said *Sibboleth:* for he could not frame to pronounce it right. Then they took him and slew him at the passages of the Jordan."

This Bible story (Judges, 12:6) explains the presence of the Hebrew word *shibboleth* in present-day English. When first borrowed, its meaning was "password," but it has since come to mean any characteristic peculiar to a minority group. (In Hebrew it is a homonym, meaning both "river, flood," and "ear of corn.")

The Gileadites may have been the first to use linguistic tests to ferret out an enemy, but they weren't the last.

Frenchmen who, during the Middle Ages, had occupied Sicily long enough to speak its Italian dialect almost perfectly, betrayed their nationality when the Sicilians revolted and put suspected enemies to the test of pronouncing *Cicero Ceci.* The French have great difficulty with the *ch*-sound, so what should have come out as "Cheechero Chee-Chee" came out instead as "Sheeshero She-She" – and spelled curtains.

The Turks, in their 19th century war with Egypt, used the Arabic word *gamal* to sift out Egyptians from captives claiming to be Syrians. Although both speak Arabic, Syrians say "jamal" instead of "gamal."

In World War II, *lallapalooza* was used to distinguish between the Japanese and other Orientals. Spoken by the Japanese, who has no *l* in his alphabet, the word comes out "rarraparooza." (The Chinese, on the other hand, have a reverse tendency. By that linguistic pressure known as lallation, they turn *r* to *l*. Ask a Chinese to say *rarraparooza* and he'll say "lallapalooza," just as he'll say "velly good" if asked to say *very good).*

The Spanish are unable to begin a word with the sound of *s* followed by another consonantal sound. They have no trouble with *sombrero, senor,* or *siesta,* in which the *s* is followed by a vowel. But when it's followed by a consonant, they resort to *prothesis,* the tacking-on of a vowel in front of the *s.* Unable to launch right in and call a spade a *spade,* they fore-add an *e* as a springboard and call it *espada.* The same accounts for *escuela* (school), *estacion* (station), *esfera* (sphere), *esqui* (ski), *especia* (spice), *Espana* (Spain), and many other Spanish *es-* words.

We English speakers shouldn't allow ourselves to be amused by others' linguistic hobblements. We have a few shibboleths of our own. That most proper *King's English*man who smiles at the Chinese "velly" does so because he finds it *veddy* — even *teddibly* — quaint.

By the way, how do you pronounce *colonel?*

'catty-cornered'

(the dice were loaded)

In Norman England there was a popular dice game in which a roll of nine took the money. The game was called *Novem,* the Latin word for "nine."

To dull the claws of Lady Luck, the dice were sometimes "loaded" so that neither of them could turn up a three or a four.

This deception was called "bar'd cater-tra," a corrupted mixture of the English word *barred* and the French words *quatre,* four, and *trois,* three. With the three and four "barred," one might roll the dice until the end of time without rolling a nine.

This sense of endlessness, of rolling on and on, was used by Dekker in *The Honest Whore* (1604): "I have suffered your tongue, like a *bar'd cater-tra,* to run all the while."

Cater also showed up in the now obsolete expression *cater-cousin.* Literally meaning quarter-cousin or fourth-cousin, it was used to deny relationship rather than to claim it. To say that a person was a cater-cousin was a way of saying he was "just a friend."

There also was the term *cater-cornered,* which survives today as "catty-cornered." Something that sits catty-cornered sits "on the quarter," or on the diagonal.

'ache'

(Dr. Sam took the wrong road)

In early English, there was an interesting handful of verbs which ended with the *k*-sound while their corresponding noun forms finished off with *ch.* For example, in modern spelling:

speak	speech
make	match
stick	stitch
wake	watch
stink	stench
bake	batch
break	breech

And, if Dr. Samuel Johnson hadn't taken a wrong turn in his *Dictionary,* we could add to this little list —

ake	ache ("aitch")

In Middle English, *ake* was indeed the spelling of that verb we now treat as *ache.* "Lat our hedes nevere ake," prayed Chaucer. And, conforming to the *k:ch* tradition, the corresponding noun was spelled *ache* and pronounced "aitch." In those days, a head that *oke* (past tense of *ake*) was a "headaitch."

Ake is o.o.o., of obscure origin. We can trace it with certainty to the Old English *aece,* present tense of *acan,* "to ache." But that's not very far, certainly not far enough for Dr. Johnson, one of those philologists who, as Cowper observed, "chase a panting

74

syllable through time and space, start it at home, and hunt it in the dark, from Gaul, to Greece, and into Noak's Ark."

Dr. Johnson didn't chase *ake* into Noah's Ark, but he did chase it to Greece. That may have been the right direction, but if it was, the good doctor took a wrong turn somewhere. He ascribed *ake* (in his *Dictionary,* 1755) to the Greek *axos,* meaning "to drive, to turn." He probably reasoned that an aching could be interpreted as a driving, turning, throbbing sensation. Since the *x* in *axos* is not the English *x,* but rather the Greek *chi* which represents the palatal *ch* or *k*-sound, Dr. Johnson concluded that *ake,* the verb, should be spelled *ache.*

By that time, popular usage had already converted the pronunciation of the noun from "aitch" to "ake," and with Dr. Johnson's dictum, both noun and verb settled down as *ache,* pronounced "ake." Let's hope they stay that way.

'stream'

(it flows into embarrassing waters)

Say "sream."
A little hard to say?
Try "stream."
Easier? Right. And what would you say you did to make it easier? Stuck a *t* between the *s* and the *r*? That's one way of saying it. Another way is to say you epenthesized it.

Epenthesis is a linguists' term signifying the insertion of a consonant between two other consonants "to facilitate transition from one to the other." In other words, it's hard to say "sream" because it's hard to go, phonetically, from *s* to *r*. But it's easy to go from *s* to *t* and easy to go from *t* to *r,* so "stream" is no trouble.

Of course, it never would have been any trouble if the "Indo-Europeans" had left their word *roum* alone. But there was an Indo-European tendency to intensify certain words by prefixing an *s*-sound, and because of this, *roum,* meaning "a flowing," became *sroum.*

Some descendant languages had no difficulty with *sroum.* It developed into the Sanskrit *sravati,* Celtic *srutu,* Old Irish *sruth,* and the Lithuanian *srove,* all meaning "stream" or "flowing."

But the Germanic looked for an easier way. And found it. By epenthesis it converted *sroumos* into *straumoz*, which is the primitive Germanic precursor of the modern English *stream*.

The Greek language had an even easier way. It simply knocked the *s* off *sroum* and wound up with *rheuma*, a flowing, and *rhein*, to flow. Thanks to *rheuma*, runny noses and watery eyes are said to be *rheumy*. Thanks to *rhein*, we have the *rhoid* of *hemorrhoid*, a flowing of blood, and the *rhea* of *diarrhea*, a flowing through, and *gonorrhea*, a flowing of semen, and what this proves is that if you follow *stream* to its source, it will take you into some embarrassing waters.

'pygmy'

(his name tells you how big he is)

The man who is professionally handy with his fists is called a *pugilist*. The word derives from the Latin *pugil*, which is closely related to Latin *pugnus*, meaning "fist." Whence, incidentally, the word *pugnacious*.

The Greek equivalent of *pugnus* was *pugme*. This noun produced the adjective, *pugmaios*, meaning "fist-sized."

The Greeks from the time of Homer knew of a race of miniature Africans, whom they described in their poetry and on their vases, and whom they named *Pugmaios*.

The Latin language borrowed the name, altering it to *Pygmaeus*, and that's the origin of the word *pygmy*. A pygmy, literally, is "about as big as your fist."

'bosom'

(what's *titte* for the Danes is *tatte* for the Swedes)

Man has availed himself of numerous names for the female bosom, including *bosom*. There is some doubt about the origin of this particular title. Some philologists suggest the Indo-European root *bog*, understood to refer to "the space embraced by the arms." Others feel that a likelier origin is the Indo-European *bhas*, "to puff, swell, inflate," a theory which is supported by the Sanskrit *bhasman,* "blowing," and *bhastra,* "bellows."

The earliest origin of which we are sure is the West Germanic *bosm,* Old Frisian *bosem,* Old English *bosm,* which in Middle English took the present spelling, *bosom.*

The Latin *papilla,* breasts, has contributed the English *pap,* Swedish *pappe,* French *poupe,* and Italian *poppa,* all meaning breasts or bosom, and *bubbie* is an American spelling of the English *bubby,* which itself is borrowed from the German *bubbi.*

When a woman speaks of her *bust,* she refers to only a part of what the word originally defined, i.e., the whole torso.

We can trace the word *bust* through the French *(buste)* and Italian *(busto)* to the Latin *bustum,* but there the etymology becomes hazy:

Bustum was a Latin word for "tomb," over which sculptured busts of the occupants were placed.

There also was the Latin *busta, busca,* meaning "log", and with this sense of tree-*trunk* the word may have transferred to the *trunk* of the body.

To confuse things further, there was the later Latin word *busta,* meaning a small box, or *chest.*

For *teat* and *tit* we go back to the Germanic *titta,* which had such cognates as the Armenian *tit* and Greek *titthe.* This Germanic prototype is believed to be the origin of the Romance equivalents, French *tette,* Spanish *teta,* Italian *tetta,* as well as the Danish *titte,* Swedish *tatte,* Dutch *tit,* and Old English *titt* and *tit.* The Middle English spelling, *teat,* is due to the influence of the Middle French *tete.*

Man has attested to his admiration for this part of the female anatomy in numerous ways, not the least of which is the naming of mountains for it. The *"Great Paps of Jura,"* for example. And right here in the U.S., those eminences nobly called *Grand Tetons.* Not to mention *Pike's Peak or Bust.*

'Vietnam'

(it's Chinese for *not-Chinese*)

Viet is a very old Chinese appelation meaning "non-Chinese people." *Nam* is the Chinese word for "south." *Vietnam,* then, is a compound meaning "those foreigners to the south."

Just as North Vietnam and the Republic of South Vietnam divide the country geographically (or did up until press-time, at least), so do their dialects divide the Vietnamese language. Each dialect is known by the name of the capital of that partition where it prevails, i.e., *Hanoi Vietnamese* is spoken in the north, while *Saigon Vietnamese* is spoken in the south.

'nostril'

(and why third base is not thrid base)

Had you realized that before you can pronounce any word, your mind must send to your speech mechanism separate orders for the articulation of each of the different sounds, or syllables, in that word?

That's not all. It also must send out the orders for the sounds *in the same sequence in which those sounds are to appear in the word.*

Sometimes it gets mixed up. Sometimes it becomes preoccupied with a certain sound in a word and thus orders it up earlier than it should. When that happens, the speech organs obey instantly, crowding that sound ahead of its usual position in the word.

Consider the word *nostril*. Its Old English form was *nosthirl*. The *nos* is self-explanatory, and the *thirl* was from *thirlian*, the Old English verb meaning "to pierce, to drill, to bore." A *nosthirl*, then, was a nose-piercing, or a hole in the nose.

During the Middle English period, *thirlian* eased to *thirlen*, and then an interesting thing happened. People began saying "thrillen" instead of "thirlen." And "thrill" instead of "thirl." And "nosthril" (later *nostril*) instead of "nosthirl."

This is an example of metathesis, that phonetic bubu which occurs when the mind is unconsciously attracted to a certain sound within a word, thus commanding the speech organs to produce it prematurely.

A better example is the word *clasp*, which was *clapse* during the Middle English period. Or *wasp*, which first was *waps*. Or *lisp*, which first was *lips*. In these words, the mind, subconsciously intent on the *s*-sound, moved that sound ahead of the *p*-sound.

You've probably heard youngsters say "pasghetti" for *spaghetti.* This, too, is metathesis. And if you've ever heard someone say, "I ax you," instead of "I ask you," you've heard metathesis reversing itself. The Old English form of *ask* was indeed *aks.* Metathesis switched *aks* to *ask,* and now it occasionally switches *ask* back to *aks,* or "ax."

Metathesis, meaning "put over" or "trans-pose," is especially active with the *thr*-sound. Third base, for example, would be *thrid base* if metathesis hadn't interfered with the Old Saxon *thrid. Threshold* once was *therscold.* The Yorkshire term *riding,* referring to that county's three divisions, is a remnant of the day when "thirding" was pronounced "thriding." The Old English *throp,* "village," by metathesis became *thorp, thorpe* (and the "before and after" story of this particular word is still seen in the surnames Win*throp* and Ogle*thorpe*).

The present-day word *thrill* is a descendant of the same Old English *thirlian* mentioned above. As "a piercing," it is analagous to the expression, "sends a shiver through me." The same sense is present in "a piercing cry." Note that while *thrill* today describes an emotion that is enjoyably exciting, that hasn't always been the case. Originally it meant *any* emotional excitation, including disgust, fear, and shame. The historian, John Richard Green, wrote that when King John in 1213 surrendered his kingdom to the Roman See, receiving it back as a tributary vassal of the Pope, "England thrilled at the news with a sense of national shame such as she had never felt before."

If you want to thrill a lady, paint her with compliments, but be careful when you come to the *nose.* If you turn to the *Song of Solomon* for a few ideas, it's allright to tell her that "thy thighs are like jewels," or that "thy neck is as a tower of ivory." Or even, if you must, that "thine eyes are like the fishpools in Heshbon." But *stop right there.* Only Solomon could get away with the next line, "Thy nose is as the tower of Lebanon which looketh toward Damascus."

'cis'

(which side is this side?)

At least 90% of all high school graduates have heard the term *Cisalpine.* Of this number, the chances are (1) that 90% were not told what it means, and (2) that the same 90% never asked. It's very simple, and better late than never:

Cis is a Latin preposition meaning "on this side of."

Cisalpine, therefore, means "on this side of the Alps."

Cisequator means "on this side of the equator."

Cisatlantic means "on this side of the Atlantic."

Such adjectives, however, are not very definite definitions. Obviously, there's an ocean of difference between what Cisatlantic means to an Englishman and what it means to his American cousin.

'mice'

(why don't we say "mouses?")

There are a few nouns whose plural and singular forms are the same. Deer, for example, and sheep, and fish. And you can even get by with "a load of brick." But usually we change the word to show that it's more than one. How many of our pluralizing devices can you think of?

There's the simple s-ending, of course. 1 house + 1 house = 2 houses.

And the rarer en-ending: 1 ox + 1 ox = 2 oxen.

And for numerous plural forms, we've adopted the Latin plural ending -ia. 1 medium + 1 medium = 2 media.

But there's another pluralizer that doesn't involve the word's ending at all. It's called "the mutated plural," and the mutation takes place in the vowels of the singlular noun. Man becomes men; woman, women; foot, feet; goose, geese; tooth, teeth; louse, lice, and mouse, mice. There's no particular reason why we pluralize these seven nouns this way; we just do. If you want to say "mouses" instead of "mice," there's no law against it. Everybody will understand what you're saying. They just won't understand why you're saying it.

'*I*'

(a double dose of egotism?)

The personal pronoun *I* is a good example of the way the basic Germanic language changed the sound of *g* to that of *k* as it weaned away from the Indo-European mother tongue (see *Foreword*).

The history of *I* begins with the Indo-European *ego,* which is retained in Greek and Latin but which the Germanic tongue converted to *eka.*

With its *e* unstressed, *eka* became *ika.* As different Germanic sub-languages developed, *ika* dropped its final vowel,* appearing in Gothic and Old Frisian as *ik* and in Old Saxon and Old English as *ic.* In Middle High German it became *ich,* a form it keeps in modern German.

Ic remained *ic* during the Old English period, with less and less stress on the *c.* During the Middle English period, this consonant dropped away entirely. With its departure there came a restressing of the remaining *i*-sound and the resultant "eye" pronunciation we know today.

With *ego* so prominent in its ancestry, *I* can be pardoned for a certain amount of egotism. But it seems to have gotten an unearned double dose. How else can we account for the fact that of the whole team of pronouns — I, you, he, she, it, we, us, they, them, etc. — *I* is the only one that's always capitalized?

'*take*'

(or, why English is Greek to the Chinese)

The Anglo-Saxons took the word *take* from the Old Norse *taka.* This is fortunate. We'd have a hard time saying what we mean without it. And it's equally fortunate that we grow up knowing how to handle it. If we had to learn, from a textbook, we'd be climbing walls. For instance:

*A common linguistics characteristic known as *apocope,* the dropping off of final syllables.

We say, "If you want to give it to me, I'll take it." But we also say, "If you don't give it to me, I'll take it." Imagine what that does to a poor Chinese trying to learn English.

If you take somebody in, you either cheat him or give him a home. If you take somebody on, you either fight him or give him a job. If you take up for somebody, you defend him, but if you take over, you grab control.

You take time, take charge, take castor oil, take issue, take communion, take shelter, take offense, take pity and take guitar lessons.

If you take a liking to a lady, take her out to the old ball game. If somebody tries to take her away, take a swing at him; if he takes you to court you can take the Fifth Amendment.

Some things are easy to take, others are hard to take. If you can take it, fine. If you can't take it, you can take tranquillizers. Or take to drink. Or even take arsenic — but don't do *that;* just take it easy and things will take a turn for the better.

You take a bath, take a vow, take a trip, take hold, take a snapshot, take a taxi, take a nap, take a tumble, take tea, take sugar in it, take a magazine, take a look, take a left turn and take a hint. If you're photogenic, you take a good picture; of you're not, you can take cover. You take a break, take an option, take a day off, take a back road, take advice, take a beating, take heart, take a seat, take a stand, and — *gesundheit* — take a cold. Got enough? Okay, take off. But take care of yourself. And don't take any wooden nickels.

'bastard'

(and other h-*ard* language)

Hilaire Belloc wrote a captivating poem about a medieval French inn where the girls went glancing, chancing, dancing, backing and advancing.

The young muleteers who were always passing through liked to come and join in the fun. But as Belloc pointed out, they weren't spending a penny because they hadn't any. Didn't even have a room at the inn. Instead, they slept on their pack-saddles, with maybe a little straw from the stable.

It sometimes happened that one of these young muleskinners found a girl willing to retire with him to his pack-saddle. If she subsequently bore a child, it was called a *bastard* — a term which half-explains itself when we know that the Old French word for pack-saddle was *bast*.

The other half of the word, *-ard*, is an Old French suffix from the Old High German *hard, hart*, meaning bold, severe, hard. It added the meaning "severely so," "done to excess." The hard drinker was a drunk*ard*. One who was excessively slow, sluggish or lagging, was a slugg*ard* or a lagg*ard*. An overly stupid fellow was a dull*ard*, and one in his dotage was a dot*ard*. The variant form, from *hart*, is seen in bragg*art*.

Since *-ard* was seldom used to describe any *good* thing done to excess, it became associated with discreditable things. This is the meaning it attached to *bast;* it was no great credit to be a pack-saddle baby.

Bastard, meaning illegitimate, is muleskinners' language.

But then, who has a more legitimate right to it?

(it's kin to *Cosa Nostra*)

Although the Arabians didn't invent algebra, they pioneered so much in its development that it's generally regarded as an Arabian product.

But its best-known symbol, the *x* which stands for the unknown quantity in algebra, was never known to the Arabians.

Instead, they used the Arabic word *shei*, which meant *thing* in the sense of "a *something*."

The Greeks, during the Middle Ages, transcribed *shei* as *xei*. This was not a spelling *of* the Greek word *xi*, the name of the symbol we English-speakers call "ex." It was a spelling *with* that other Greek letter *chi*, which, written as *x*, represents the hard *ch*-sound, as in *cholera*. Thus the Greek transliteration of the Arabic *shei* was written *xei* and pronounced "kei."

The name *algebra* is an early Italian spelling of the Arabic *al jebr,* itself an ellipsis of *al jebr wa al moqabalah,* meaning "the restoration and the comparison." This term is explained by the Arabians' interpretation of algebra as the comparing of separate parts so they might be restored as a whole. (The same word, *al jebr,* was their name for bone-setting, i.e., the restoring of broken parts).

The Italians had another name for algebra, *regola di cosa.* It meant "rule of the coss," or "rule of *something,*" "rule of *x.*" *Cosa* is the Italian word for "thing," as in the name of that great American enterprise, Cosa Nostra, which restores broken people and broken laws into high living and Swiss bank accounts.

'buxom'

(which brides once vowed they'd be)

"If the bough breaks, the cradle will fall."

So warns the old lullabye.

But the bough, if it lives up to its name, is not likely to break. It will bend, bend like a bow — *bow* being a variant of *bough,* which comes from the Old English *bugan,* "to bend, to yield."

Bough (bow) led to the adjective *boughsome (bowsome),* which meant "yielding, pliant, tractable, agreeable." Or, one might say, "obedient," which was what Fitz-Herbert had in mind when he wrote, redundantly, "I shall be buxsome and obedient to justices."

But notice his spelling, *buxsome.* It is a perfect bridge for the gap between *boughsome* and *buxom. Buxom* you see, originally had the same meaning as *boughsome,* yielding, pliant, agreeable.

Gradually it came to suggest a different kind of yielding — the plump, pliant female curves which men thought yielded most agreeably to the touch.

Dr. Sam Johnson attributed this change in meaning to the suggestiveness of the old English marriage ceremony, in which every bride took her vow to be "obedient and buxom in bed and board."

It cannot be denied, the more a lady has to yield, the more she is capable of yielding. The more buxom the squaw, the more bucksome the buck.

'adultery'

(there's no nourishment in it)

Ask ten average persons and about nine of them will say that the words *adult* and *adultery* are related. This proves the majority is not always right.

Adult is from the Latin *adultus,* which itself is a derivant of *adolescere,* "to grow up." This verb, the origin also of *adolescent,* comes from the older form, *alere,* which meant to nourish, in the sense of "to rear," "to bring up."

Adultery has an entirely different origin. It's from the Latin *adulterare,* a coinage, probably, from the phrase *"ad alterum se conferre,"* meaning to betake one's self to another.

At one time, the word for one who committed adultery was *adulter.* This noun came to be used also as a verb. To avoid confusion a second *-er* was added to the noun, hence *adulterer.* The old adjective, *adulterine,* has been replaced by *adulterous* (as has *adulterize* by *adulterate*).

Etymologically, then, any identification of *adult* with *adultery* is a case of mistaken identity. The mistake is understandable. The word called *adult* may have nothing to do with adultery, but the *people* called adults have quite a bit to do with it. Those called juveniles, too, it would seem.

'folk etymology'

(Eve was neither helpmeet nor helpmate,
music hath no charms to soothe a savage
beast, and five-gallon hats don't hold
five gallons)

One little boy told another that a certain farmer was called Barney because he had a barn.

One of my own sons, when he was a tyke, overheard the name Horace Greeley and asked whether Mr. Greeley rode horses.

Many persons, asked unexpectedly for the meaning of the word *walnut,* will immediately think of "wall-nut." Others think of varicose veins as "very coarse veins." A child says "ice cream comb" because he's familiar with the word *comb* but not with *cone.*

All of us, consciously and unconsciously, search for the meaning of an unknown word by associating that word with others which bear some resemblance and whose meanings we know.

And in doing so, sometimes make seemingly logical leaps to the most illogical conclusions, which, if presented to others, then become *folk etymology.*

Various Explanations

Folk etymology is always *false* etymology, but there are varying explanations for it.

Sometimes it's innocently false, as in the case of Cinderella's slippers, in which people understandably confused the French words *fuere* (fur) and *verre* (glass).

Sometimes it comes with tongue in cheek, as in the threadbare example of *sirloin,* the word which has been attributed to three different English kings who so loved this particular cut of beef that it was knighted *Sir Loin.* (Since the word is a variant of *surloin,* from the French *sur-longe,* "above the loin," it matters little whether the credit is given to Henry VIII, James I, or Charles II).

Sometimes folk etymology is disgustingly irresponsible, as in the case of a contemporary writer who (1) explained the place-name *Waterbury* as a spot where bodies were buried in the water and (2) is old enough to know better.

And sometimes it's carelessly false, as in "Music hath charms to soothe the savage beast," which made more sense the way William Congreve wrote it, "Music hath charms to soothe a savage *breast.*"

Equally careless is the widespread and still spreading "chaise *lounge.*" The correct term, of course, is "chaise *longue,*" French for "long chair." But the chaise longue looks quite loungey, and *longue* looks quite like *lounge,* and that's all the encouragement folk etymology ever needs.

"Five-Gallon" Hats

In medieval England, a *galoon* was a closely woven ribbon or braid, usually with gold, silver, or silk threads, used to trim apparel. Said the lady, Jug, in *Pills To Purge Melancholy,*

> "A wheel, six platters and a spoon,
> a jacket, edg'd with blue *galoon.*"

The word, spelled *galloon* in modern dictionaries, came from the Norman French *galon,* Old French *jalon.* Its origin beyond that is obscure, but it probably came from Vulgar Latin (see *'Vulgar Latin',* preceding) since it shows up in other Romance languages, e.g., Italian *gallone,* Spanish *galon.*

It's the Spanish word that we're interested in. As that language came through Mexico to the American Southwest, there came with it *sombreros,* men's hats with tall crowns. The taller the crown, the more *galons,* or fancy hatbands, the hat would accommodate. Some were five-*galon* hats, some went as high as ten *galons.* And today we assume that the term is five-*gallon,* or ten-*gallon* — a bit of folk etymology aided and abetted, perhaps, by movies in which cowboys water their horses from their hats.

No Helpmeet, Eve

In the King James Version of the Bible, *Genesis 2:18* tells us:

> "And the Lord God said, It is not
> good that man should be alone; I
> will make him an help meet for him."

Notice that *help* and *meet* are two words here. Also that God didn't say, "I will make him an help meet" — He said "I will make him an help *meet* for him." Or, as the Revised Standard Version translates this same passage, "I will make him an helper *fit* for him."

Meet, now archaic, is a subsequent form of the Middle English *mete,* which meant "fit, fitting," or "as befits." It is the same *mete* seen in the Biblical admonition,"As ye mete, so shall it be measured unto you." But folk etymology, cheered on by the common budgetary expression, "make ends meet," read the words *help meet* as a compound *helpmeet.* And then, deciding that *mate* was what God had really intended to say, gave birth to the term help*mate.*

When the Moon Comes Over the Pentis

What's so pent about a penthouse?

Does the *pent* mean "pent up?"

Or does it somehow relate to the Greek word for "five," as in *Pentagon?*

Possibly it comes from *pentelic,* referring to that township in ancient Attica which was the origin of the word *attic?*

No, none of these. It comes from the same word *appendix* comes from — the Latin *appendare,* "to hang from" — via the Medieval French *appentis* and the Middle English *appentice, appentis,* meaning "appendage."

Those medieval Englishmen who were fortunate enough to own a cow usually built a cowshed right onto their houses. Any such kind of appendage was an *appentis,* but thanks to aphesis (the dropping of first syllables, e.g., *esquire, squire; appall, pall*) the popular name became *pentis.* Later, when men wondered about this odd name for a shed, they fell into folk etymology's trap. Remembering that *backus* was a colloquial form of *bak(e)house,* as were *bellus* of bellhouse and *barkus* of barkhouse (tannery), and aided by the logic that a *pentis* was a sort of house, they simply "corrected" the word to *penthouse.*

A Touchy Subject

The modern word *touchy* is totally unrelated to the word *touch.*

It started as *techy,* a perfectly legitimate word meaning peevish, irritable, which can be found today in any respectable dictionary.

But it sounded like "tetchy," from "tetch," the bumpkin mispronunciation of *touch.* And so folk etymology, intending only to be helpful and encouraged by the image of a person who would be irritated if so much as touched, "corrected" *techy* to *touchy.*

From 'modest' to 'ashamed'

The word *shamefast* derives from the Old English *sceamfaest,* meaning "modest, shy."

This meaning is exemplified in the Coverdale Bible passage, "If thy daughter be not shamefast, holde her straitly," which was to say, "If thy daughter be not *modest,* hold her strictly."

But *shamefast,* in which the element *fast* wasn't quite clear, sounded like shame-*faced,* which was perfectly clear. And so folk etymology allowed *shamefast,* "modest," to change to *shame-faced,*" ashamed, guilty-looking, embarrassed."

Rakehell and others

The Old English word *rakel* meant "reckless." Folk etymology converted it to *rakehell,* which then was shortened to *rake,* a word that survives today to describe one who lives dissolutely.

Wormwood has nothing to do with worm or wood. It's a bit of fiction born of the Old English *wermod,* a kind of absinthe.

Buttonhole is folk etymology. The word originally was *buttonhold,* i.e., that which holds the button.

Because of the meanings of *pro,* for, and *anti,* against, folk etymology generally considers a *protagonist* to be the opposite of an *antagonist.* This is hardly the case; a *protagonist* is one who plays a leading role, a first or prime role, from the Greek *protos,* first, and *agonistes,* actor.

Welsh rabbit is a tongue-in-cheek name for a dish that has no rabbit in it, but folk etymology for years has been taking the word seriously, and as a consequence still tries to persuade us that the proper term is *Welsh rarebit.*

Alibi is understood to mean any kind of excuse, but this isn't so. Its real meaning is limited to the excuse that one was *not at a certain place at a certain time.*

Try yourself on this one:

Why are tweezers called *tweezers?*

Doesn't the concept of "squeezers," pinchers, come to mind? Maybe with a tinge of "tweaker?"

It does with most people, but *tweezers* derives from the French *etuis*, the name of the case in which such instruments were carried, pronounced "etwee" and "twee."

Walnut is related to *Welsh* and *Wales*, but not to *wall*. It derives ultimately from *Volcae*, the name of a powerful Celtic people in Gaul. This name, pronounced "Wolcae," is the origin of the Old English word *wealh* and the German *welsch*, meaning "stranger" hence "foreigner." The adjective of *wealh* is *welisc*, whence the national adjective, *Welsh*. A walnut, from the Old English *wealh hnuta*, Middle English *walnote*, is simply a "foreign nut."

Belfry, or *belfrey*, has nothing to do with *bell*. It comes from *bervrit*, a movable tower which could be filled with men and shoved against the wall of a fortress under attack, thus protecting them until the very moment they leaped onto the top of the wall. As *bervrit*, a compound of the Middle High German *bergen*, "conceal," and *vride*, "protection, peace," developed into the English *belfrey*, it took on the meaning of any kind of tower. The bells came later and are coincidental. As a matter of fact, *bell* wasn't even the word for the bell we know today until much later.

You get a line, I'll get a pole, we'll go down to the *crefis'* hole. *Crawfish*, or *crayfish*, is unrelated to *fish*. The Old High German word for "crab" was *krebiz*. The Old French borrowed it as *ecrevisse*. This became the English *crefis*, *crevis*, which folk etymology has interpreted as "crayfish."

Not all folk etymology, or *false* etymology, catches on.

If it did, the word *curmudgeon*, meaning an ill-tempered, cantankerous fellow, might today have somewhat the meaning of *anonymous*. This premise, expose as it does the clay feet of scholasticism, is based on an incident which may forever after give philologists a great chuckle and chortle:

It was no secret, in the early 1750's that the great Samuel Johnson was at work on the first English dictionary. He invited qualified help. There must have been those who knew he was uncertain about the origin of the word *curmudgeon*, or that he would be interested in it, for he seems to have received an unsigned letter saying that the word derives (as it possibly does) from the French *couer mechant*, "wicked heart." Having no better explanation of his own, Dr. Johnson in his *Dictionary* referred to the word as "a vitious manner of pronouncing *couer mechant*," adding, "Fr. an unknown correspondent."

90

But the lexicographer John Ash, LL. D., when he published his own dictionary some twenty years later, interpreted Dr. Johnson's "Fr." as an abbreviation of *French,* not of *from* as Johnson intended. Accordingly, he defined *curmudgeon* as "from the French *couer,* unknown, and *mechant,* a correspondent."

This reveals in Dr. Ash either a shameful carelessness or a deplorable ignorance of French. It also questions the fastidiousness of Dr. Johnson in capitalizing, mid-sentence, the word *from.* But as every man who presumes to write about language should be the first to insist, to err is human and to forgive is divine. Or, as it is writ:

> There's so much good in the worst of us,
> And so much bad in the best of us,
> That it hardly behooves any of us
> To chuckle and chortle at the rest of us.

'biscuit'

(not what it used to be)

The *bis* in *biscuit* is really *bi,* the familiar old prefix standing for two or twice, as in *bicycle, bi-monthly,* etc. In *biscuit* it signifies twice-baked — or, more literally, twice-cooked, the *-cuit* coming from the French *cuire,* to cook.

The identical meaning is represented by *zweiback,* a compound of the German *zwei,* two, and *back,* bake.

These biscuits were simply breads baked to be re-baked or, if you will, "warmed up." Not at all like today's biscuits. Which usually, of course, is no great loss.

Zwei is a High German, or *Hochdeutsch,* word. It is a good example of the fact that High German is much less like English than is Low German, or *Plattdeutsch,* as in these comparisons:

ENGLISH	LOW GERMAN	HIGH GERMAN
two	twe	zwei
door	door	tur
tooth	tan	zan
what	wat	was
day	dag	tag
book	bok	buch
foot	foot	fuss

'cobweb'

(from a cup of poison)

There were no spiders in England until the Middle English period, sometime after 1100.

Billions of attercops, yes, but not a single *spider*. The word *spider* hadn't been born. (This is a technicality, but let me have it; technicality is the stuff of which laws are made).

Attercop was the Old English word for that eight-legged and usually eight-eyed arachnid we know today as the *spider*. *Atter*, or *attor*, meant venom, poison, and *cop* meant cup. An attercop was "a cup of poison." In time the word was shortened to *cop*, which later eased to *cob*. Hence *cobweb*, or spider-web.

The Old English word meaning "to spin" was *spinnan*. From this there came *spinthre* or *spinther*, "spinner," which during the Middle English period did some easing of its own. It became *spithre*, *spither*, and then *spider*.

Spider eventually displaced *cob*, but *spider-web* didn't displace *cobweb*. For a good reason. Whereas the spider and the cob were the same thing, the spider-web and the cobweb are two different things. The cobweb has an extra ingredient. Any spider can spin us a spider-web, but if we want a cobweb, we have to supply our own dust.

'its'

Thomas Chatterton was a young literary fraud who gave himself away with the word *its.*

He lived in the 18th century, and he'd found a way to add a profitable antique value to his poems by passing them off as the work of an imaginary 15th century monk. What tripped him up was this line:

"Life and its goods I scorn."

There's nothing wrong with this sentence today.

Nor was there anything wrong with it in 1777.

But Thomas Chatterton, remember, claimed that it was written in the 1400's.

There was no such form as *its* that early. Instead, writers of that early day used the neuter possessive pronoun *his.* If *his* looks masculine rather than neuter, the following will explain it:

In Old English, nouns and pronouns had both gender and declension. The neuter pronoun was declined *hit, his, him, hit.* Early in the Middle English period, the dative and accusative cases merged, and the declension became *hit, his, hit.* Gradually *hit* weakened to *it* as the usual form for subject and object.

But the possessive, *his,* lingered on. This explains why Portia said, "How far that little candle throws *his* beams" — not *"its* beams." Literature is full of such examples, as again, in John Donne's "Love mysteries in souls do grow, but yet the body is *his* book." And in Biblical translations, such as, "if the salt have lost *his* savor, wherewith shall it be salted?"

As you can imagine, *his* neuter and *his* masculine, with an identical-ness that destroyed their power to designate gender, caused many problems. As a result, writers began avoiding the neuter *his.* They sought various substitutes, one of which was the use of *it* as a possessive, as in Horatio's reference to the ghost in *Hamlet,* "It lifted up *it* head."

Sometimes the concept of possession was strengthened with the word *own,* as in ". . .leave it, without more mercy, to *it own* protection" (*The Winter's Tale*).

It was natural that the *apostrophe-plus-s* which made other nouns possessive — *king's, world's, John's* — should lend itself to it. Which it did. *It's* with an apostrophe, as a possessive, was used at least as early as 1597. This usage continued for almost 200 years, and undoubtedly would be the proper form today but for the coincidence that finally drove the apostrophe out but left the *s*:

As *it's,* it conflicted with the identically-written colloquial form of *it is.*

Something had to go.

What went was the apostrophe, leaving *its* as the neuter possessive we use today.

For authenticity's sweet sake, Tom Chatterton's line should have read, "Life and *his* goods I scorn," and that's what tripped him up. Exposed as a fraud, poor penniless Tom took poison. He was only seventeen years old. Considering his age, he was a genius, and it's tragic that he died so early. Tragic that he lived so early, too, because some of his work was so obscene it couldn't be published. Think what a literary giant that'd make him today.

'hit'

(and why Devil Anse Hatfield
called his sons "babbies")

"December 13, 1887

"Dear Sir: *Inclosed* please find fifteen dollars to pay *feese* due your office upon the issue of state warrants for the following named *Parteys,* warrant for Anderson Hatfield, Johnson Hatfield, Cap Hatfield, Daniel Whitt, Albert McCoy (Kirk's *sone*). . .Some of the other Parteys is dead and some *gon* and left the *contery*. . .Just *copyed* the indictment so if we want any others. . .we will send for the warrants *heare* after.

"Yours *respectly,*
Frank Phillips."

This communication, written many years ago to West Virginia's Governor E. W. Wilson, is about as "legal" as any evidence we'll find to support the declaration that Appalachian mountaineers use an Elizabethan vintage of English — or did until recent years when highways and factory jobs began luring them out into the world.

Each word italicized was, somewhere in England at some time during or before the Middle English period, written just as it appears in Frank Phillips' letter. *Inclose,* according to the Oxford English Dictionary, was "the legal and statutory form" of *enclose.* The word *gon* is the Middle English development of the Old English *gan.* Other words show the characteristic use of *y* for *i,* and the Middle English *e*-ending is much in evidence, in *"feese", "heare"* and *"sone".*

In speaking of his "sones", Anderson "Devil Anse" Hatfield, leader in his family's feud with the McCoys, used another Middle English form which appears several times in John L. Spivak's account of the feud, *The Devil's Brigade*:

"'I want this hyar trouble settled,' Anse resumed quietly. 'Nobody likes to always be a-worryin' about his wife and *babbies.*'" And again, when officers came searching for his son, Cap Hatfield: "I ain't a-huntin' no trouble. I've hed enough fur a lifetime. But the man that hurts my *babby* hurts me."

Although Devil Anse might have been the only man bold enough to call a Hatfield a "babby," this was indeed a Middle English dialectal pronunciation of *baby.* Similarly, "bab" during the 14th and 15th centuries was a dialectal form of *babe* (as Shakespeare indicated by rhyming *babe* with *slab* and *drab*).

Jim Comstock's inimitable mountain newspaper, *The West Virginia Hillbilly,* recently reported that "a sweet-talking man sweet-talked her into playing house with him, and being *clever,* as they say in our hills, she gave of herself freely." *Clever* in Elizabethan England meant "nimble of claws, sharp to seize." Kin to the Middle English *clivers,* "claws," it softened during the early 18th century to mean "amiable, quick to agree," subsequently picking up its present-day meaning, "sharp-witted."

The West Virginia Hillbilly also spoke of "scraping a hanover," thereby using a little-known synonym for the turnip-like rutabaga that goes back to the first King George. (He and subsequent sovereigns of the Hanoverian line were less than loved in the east of England, especially in Suffolk. This gave rise to the Suffolk expression, "Go to Hanover and hoe turnips!," an invitation roughly equivalent to "Go to hell and shovel ashes!")

But of all the vestiges of early English which have found sanctuary in the Appalachian backhills, none is as widespread and tenacious as *hit*. This word goes even beyond Elizabeth and the Middle English period, back to the salad days of Old English, when *he, heo* and *hit* were the Anglo-Saxon forms of *he, she* and *it*.

Who really started the Hatfield-McCoy feud? Stranger, hit's best not to bryng that uppe.

'sex'

(united we stand, divided we multiply)

"Ameobas at the start
Were not complex;
They tore themselves apart
And started Sex."

There's as much truth as poetry in this delightful little quatrain by the late Arthur Guiterman.

The word *sex* comes directly from the Latin *secare*, meaning to separate, to cut or pull apart, to divide as amoebas do.

By dividing, we get *sections* — for example, those sections of England known as Es*sex*, Wes*sex*, Sus*sex* and Middle*sex*.

Section, of course, is an extension of *sect*, which also means a division. And which moonlights as a verb, e.g., the geometric *bisect* and anatomical *dissect*.

Secare also provides the word *insect*, a reference to the way the typical bug seems to be sectioned: "Well may they be called 'insects,'" wrote Pliny the Elder, "by reason of those cuts and divisions which some have about the neck, others in the breast and belly, the which do go around and part the members of the body."

The etymological meaning of *sex*, therefore, is simply "division." If anyone should ask what the *un*-etymological meaning is, pay him no mind. One who has to ask such a question will not believe the answer.

'mush!'

(a Gallic giddy-ap)

When those frostbitten trappers and Mounties climb onto the tailgates of their dogsleds, they always yell "Mush!" Every movie-goer knows this. But why *"mush?"* Why not *"Giddy-ap"* or *"Let's go"* or anything but *mush?*

As a matter of fact, "Let's go" is what they *do* yell, but they yell it in French. "Mush" is short for "Mushons," which is a corruption of the *marchons,* meaning "Let us walk," or, figuratively, "Let's get this thing on the road."

(The other *mush,* which began as a name for a thick porridge made of mashed corn and now defines any soft, yielding, "mushy" mass, is a dialectal variant of the noun, *mash.)*

'onion'

(a pearl-like *one*-ion)

When we regard the word *onion* as *"one"-ion,* the meaning of *union* is quite clear. A union of layers, successive skins adding up to one-ness, that's what *onion* means.

The word comes from the Latin *unio,* union, which in turn derives from the Latin *unus,* one.

A pearl develops the same way an onion grows, layer on layer, and for that reason *unio* was the Roman word for *pearl.*

The onion is growing very fast as a convenience food. There was a time when just a glance at a woman with knife in hand and tears streaming down her face, and you knew she'd been peeling onions.

Nowadays the onions come already peeled and chopped, in little boxes and jars. Nowadays if you see a weeping woman with a knife in her hand, you'd better call the police. She's probably stabbed her husband.

'English'

(and why fishermen are called anglers)

The primitive Germanic *ang* produced such derivants as the Old Norse *ongull* and the Old Saxon, Old High German and Old English *angul*, all meaning "hook."

These words were closely related to the Greek *ankulos* and Latin *angulus*, both meaning "a bend," and to the Sanskrit *anka*, "hook." The Latin *ancora*, borrowed from the Greek *ankura*, became the Old French *ancre*, which developed into the Old English *ancor*, the name of that hook we know today as *anchor*.

This explains why fishing is called *angling*. It's "hooking."

If you'll open an atlas to *Germany*, you'll see at the tip-top a little nub called Schleswig-Holstein. At one time, Schleswig was a dominion unto itself. It curved around the east and north of the little nub, like a hook, and was called "The Angle of Schleswig." The people who lived there were known as Angles, Engles and Ingles, variations which survive in the French *Anglais*, German *Englisch*, and Italian *Inglese*, all meaning "English."

At that time when the Angles joined their North Germanic cousins, the Jutes and Saxons, on the big island across the North Sea, the island was known as *Brittania*. This was a latinization, thanks to the Romans who previously had occupied the island for centuries, of the Greek *Bretanoi*. It survived as the Old English *Breoten*, Middle English *Bretayne*, modern *Britain*.

After the arrival of the Angles, Jutes, and Saxons, there developed *Angla-land* and *Engle-land* and, eventually, *England* as the name for all of the island except what we know today as Wales and Scotland. Meanwhile, *English*, literally meaning "hookish," became the name for the language spoken there.

This tongue, of course, has been influenced by many other languages, including French, Greek, Scandinavian and, to some small degree, Celtic. And *Latin* — don't forget Latin. It's a very important language. The man who doesn't know Latin should study it. It'll learn him English.

'—ia'

(a very big little suffix)

Anglia is another term for England, as is *Brittania* for Britain. These are examples of the busy little suffix — *ia* at work, and there are thousands more.

Principally a Latin/Greek borrowing, this suffix adds two rather closely related meanings which can be represented as (1) *land of, place of, home of,* and (2) *field of, area of, subject of.*

In the first sense, — *ia* is seen in *Anglia,* "place of the Angles." Also in Germania, Russia, Italia, Scandinavia, Rumania, Czechoslovakia, Austria, Arabia, Nigeria, and many others. Including, to come a bit closer to home, Virginia, Pennsylvania, Georgia, and District of Columbia. In this sense, — *ia* has a rather concrete connotation.

In the second sense, it applies more abstractly, connotes more of a generality. For example, *bacchanalia, anesthesia, mania, memorabilia, reptilia, militia, phobia.*

Note that this suffix is not to be confused with the common Latin plural ending, as in *regalia, paraphernalia, trivia,* etc. Which sometimes is very easy to do. *Mammalia,* no one can deny, is the Latin plural of *mammal.* But in English we use *mammals* as the plural and leave *mammalia* free to signify the general class of, study of, field of, mammals.

'cacafuego'

(blame it on Sir Francis Drake)

After attacking Cadiz and Lisbon in 1587, Sir Francis Drake struck a blow at the Azores. On the way he captured a valuable enemy vessel. Some say it was a Spanish galleon; others say a Portuguese carrack. No matter which, its name was *Cacafuego* and it was valued at 114,000 English pounds. Since this was about twice the cost of Drake's expedition, the news of the *Cacafuego's* capture was elating in England, and the name of the vessel quickly became well-known there. It became even better known when its meaning was learned. It was a compound of the Vulgar Latin *cacare,* to void the bowels, and the Spanish *fuego,* meaning fire. This brought into the English vernacular the now-forgotten word *cacafuego,* which was used to describe a rash, windy braggart. When translated, as it was, it brought into the vernacular still another word from which a family book like this can't get away too fast.

'janitor'

(what is so rare as a day in Iune?)

Most of us learn what a janitor is about the time we go to school. But few of us ever wonder why he's called a *janitor.* This is one of the many examples of the *i-j* kinship, by which the Latin *ianua = janua.* This word, *janua,* became the key element in janitor, i.e., doorkeeper, keeper of the keys, keeper.

In the same way, *Ianus* became *Janus,* the name of the Roman "God of the Doors." With faces on both the back and front of his head, Janus was especially built for keeping an eye on the inside while looking outside — hence the words *janiform,* "two-faced," and *janiceps,* "two-headed." January (Latin *Ienuarius, Januaris*) was so named because it is that intermediate month which "still facing Winter, also faces Spring." In January, grade school janitors enjoy looking back to last June and forward to next June.

'ab ovo'

(the egg that launched a thousand ships)

The Roman poet Stasinus had a theory about the Trojan War from which there came the Latin expression *ab ovo,* meaning "from the beginning" or, more literally, "from the egg."

Stasinus expressed his theory in *Cypria,* a lengthy bit of poetry which forms an "introduction" to Homer's *Iliad,* the story of the war between Troy and Sparta which began when Helen ran away with her lover, Paris.

But Stasinus doesn't begin with the start of the war.

He begins with the start of Helen:

Jupiter, the chief Roman god, was a determined lecher. This was no secret to Juno, his wife, who kept a very watchful eye upon him. So watchful that to deceive her, Jupiter had to take extraordinary measures.

When he wanted to spend some time with a lady known as Leda, he changed himself into a swan. Some time later and no doubt to her considerable embarrassment, Leda gave birth to a clutch of swan eggs. Helen was born of one of Leda's eggs, and that's the basis of Stasinus' *ab ovo* theory.

His reasoning is that King Menelaus of Sparta wouldn't have declared war on Troy if he hadn't been angered; that he wouldn't have been angered if his wife, Helen, hadn't run away to Troy with Paris; that Helen couldn't have run away if she hadn't been born, and that she wouldn't have been born if Leda hadn't produced that egg. Hence *ab ovo*, "from the egg."

Not daring to offend Jupiter, the egg is as far back as Stasinus dared take it. Were this not so, he'd have admitted that it all began, really, with that gleam in Jupiter's eye. A phenomenon known as the *ab Eve* theory.

'noon'

(it was three hours late)

The ancient Romans couldn't refer to the clock when speaking of the time of day, because clocks weren't invented until the 12th or 13th century. So instead of saying it was six o'clock, they said it was "the first hour."

(Note that *hour* here was not the precise sixty-minute hour we know today. The word derives from the Greek and Latin *hora*, which had the more general meaning of *season*).

Reckoning sunrise as the first "hour," the ninth hour according to the Roman method fell at about that time we know today as 3 p.m. Which, accordingly, was *nona hora*, commonly called *nona* or *nonus*, from the Latin word for "nine."

When Roman customs went to Britain with Julius Caesar, this time-telling system was among them. It took centuries for an ecclesiastical system to develop in England, but when it finally

101

did, *nonus* had a special significance. Church services were held in mid-afternoon, at that "season" of the day known as *nonus,* and the term became the popular equivalent of "churchtime."

In the 12th century, it was decided that *nonus,* or church-time, was too late in the day. Accordingly, the church hour was changed to mid-day, and in time *nonus,* later *noon,* became synonymous with mid-day or, as we say, "twelve noon."

Nonus made no impression on the Romance languages, despite their close ties to Latin. The English *noon* has the Italian equivalent *mezzogiorno;* French *midi;* Spanish *mediodia,* Portuguese *meio dia,* and Rumanian *amiaza,* all literally meaning mid-day.

'polecat'

(somewhat related to tax collectors)

In Merrie England, which had its unmerry side, a *catchpoll* was a sheriff's deputy whose job was to collect taxes. The word is a corruption of the French *chasse-poule,* "chicken-chaser," which refers to the custom of paying taxes with *poultry* when coin of the realm wasn't available.

This same *poule* accounts for the *pole* in the name of the *polecat,* which is notably fond of chickens and other poultry. *Poule* comes from the Latin *pulla,* meaning fowl or hen, which is seen also in *poult, pullet, poultry.* It comes via the Old French *pouleterie,* Middle English *pultrie,* etc.

A polecat, of course, is not a cat. But people long and whimsically have associated this little animal with felines. Skunks, for example, are frequently referred to as "kitties" and "woods-pussies." (The word *skunk,* synonymous with *polecat,* is of Algonquin Indian origin).

Philologists are uncertain about the origin of *cat.* It is represented by numerous similar words in both the Latin and Germanic languages families. According to best evidence, its ancestry is either Celtic or African, and when one knows no more than that, the subject is best dropped.

'brassiere'

(a supporting reason for its masculinity)

The French word *gorge* means "bosom" and *soutien* means "upholder." And that's all we need to understand why *soutien-gorge* is the French word for *brassiere*.

Hold on!

Isn't *brassiere* itself a French word?

Yes and no. It's a French word with an English meaning, and Victorian English at that. At times, you know, the ladies have been very prim about calling a spade a spade. Jespersen refers to "the old-fashioned prudery which prevented ladies from using such words as *leg* and *trousers*," and credits them with the invention of *fib* for that meanie, *lie*. In French, *brassiere* literally means "arm-band" or "arm-guard," from *bras*, meaning "arm." English women borrowed it, or embraced it, we might say, as a name which at the time didn't refer too pointedly to the real purpose of the garment. Or article. Or whatever.

The modern Italian word for brassiere is *riggipetto*, a compound of *petto*, breast + *riggi*, firm, rigid. In Spanish it's either *corpino*, meaning bodice, or *sosten*, meaning "prop," supporter. In German it's *bustenhalter*, which needs no defining.

English-speaking schoolkids don't know how fortunate they are. They have to learn how each word is spelled, yes, but they don't have to memorize the gender of each noun. One of the great improvements of the Middle English period was the dropping of all the genders which hobbled Old English nouns. Not so in French, Spanish, Italian and German. In those languages, all nouns are either neuter, masculine or feminine.

Oddly, in each of those languages, the nouns meaning "breast-holder" are masculine.

On second thought, maybe that isn't so odd.

'automobile'

(but for the lady in red, it might be a *mocle*)

The day will come when the electric toothbrush will be known as a *vibrodent,* or a *lectrobrush,* or something else that now seems equally ridiculous. Future generations will chuckle at us for ever having called it "electric toothbrush."

If we try to defend the name as a good way of defining a previously unknown product, our grandchildren may then demand to know why we laughed at our own grandfathers for their term *horseless carriage.* That, too, was an efficiently descriptive, perfectly reasonable name at the time, and it was used just as seriously as we now use "electric toothbrush."

But *horseless carriage,* of course, had its faults. It was long and unhandy. Besides, as descriptive as it was, it described only what *didn't* propel the carriage and failed to describe what *did* propel it. As a result, the word-coiners were soon involved in a public battle-royal for a new and better name.

The French, who had the automobile before the Americans, were calling it just that — *automobile.* With this as a cue, the sober *Scientific American* in 1895 was soberly referring to the automobile as *automobile carriage.* That same year, the *Chicago Times-Herald* sponsored a public contest whose winning name was *motocycle,* and E. P. Ingersoll, editor of a magazine called *The Horseless Age,* fought loudly for the name *motor vehicle.*

> "In England we have such heathenish abominations as 'autocar,' 'automotor,' and 'petrocar,' while in America 'motorcycle' and 'autocycle' have been set up to compete with terms already in vogue, such as 'horseless carriage,' 'motor wagon,' etc. These hasty inventions have been adopted by many editors and have attained considerable currency, but on analysis they are all found to be objectionable on one ground or another."

Meanwhile, still other "abominations" were offered the public lip. *Electrical Engineer* proposed *motor car,* and as a compromise between *motor vehicle* and *motocycle,* "another Quixote in search of a name" proposed *mocle.* Other creations included *autolocomotor, autom, horseless carriage bicycle (!), auto-wagon, polycycle, automaton,* and *autobaine,* and one inspired soul took off from the word *trolley* to coin *gasotrol, steamtrol, electrol,* and *trolibus.* Meanwhile, *automobile* was still in the running, although one magazine referred to it as "automobilious."

1899 was the year of decision. *Harper's Bazaar* reported that "Automobile Red" was a fashionable new color — a color which a reporter for *The Automobile* referred to as "Such a red as is used in the bodies of the horseless carriages driven about in Paris." Since it would be easier to hold back the dawn than to restrain women from seizing what they are told is fashionable, Automobile Red became *the* color, and the word *automobile* rode to victory on its coattails.

If it hadn't been for the ladies in red, who knows? — you might today be driving a *mocle.* Or even an *autobaine.* As the French themselves have so often advised us, *cherchez la femme.*

'mess'

(it took four persons to make one)

Of all the unappetizing names for a meal, *mess* takes the cake. Family life has rejected it for some 300 years, and only the combined might and traditions of our assorted armed services keeps it from dying an instant and unmourned death.

And yet it's a word of perfectly respectable ancestry, defiled only by the messy hand of man.

It came from the Old French *mes,* which Cotgrave (1660) defined as "a messe, or service of meat, a course of dishes at table." *Mes* was the past participle of the verb *mettre* which, along with its Latin ancestor, *mittere,* meant nothing worse than "to send, to place, to set." A *mes,* later *messe,* was simply that which was sent to the dining table. (There are various attempts to give the word other origins, such as the Spanish *mesa,* meaning "table," but these are folk etymologies to which we may pay little or no attention).

Few things get more memorably mussed, jumbled, scattered, splattered, dumped and dribbled than that which is sent to the table. Especially if the etiquette is Elizabethan, or if the diners are

105

cheered by the cup that spills, or both. As a result, *mess* was doomed also to describe any untidy, disordered, uninspiring or downright revolting bit of bleccch.

One person could not properly make a mess. Neither could two or three. Above three, there was some disagreement. "Every messe being five persons," wrote Richard Hakluyt in *Voyages, etc.,* 1589. Some time later, Thomas Heywood in *Witches of Lancastershire* wrote, "A fourth, to make us a full messe of guests." Shakespeare, in 1611, seems to have confirmed four as the proper number, with "You three fooles, lackt mee foole, to make up the messe."

'messmate'

(a meaty subject, matey)

Messmate has no connection with the word *mess,* or meal. Its initial element, *mess,* derives from the old Germanic root *maz,* which meant "meat." A *mazmate* was one who shared meat with another, just as a *companion* was one who shared bread (Latin *com,* with + *panis,* bread). The modern French word *matelot,* meaning sailor, has a similar origin. It started as *matenot,* a corruption of *maatnoot,* from the Dutch *maat,* meat + *genoot,* companion. Matelots are shipmates, ergo meatmates, ergo messmates.

'dentiscalp'

(vulgar, any way you look at it)

One of the forgotten words of the English language is *dentiscalp.* From the Latin *dentem,* tooth + *scalpere,* to scratch. "Vulgarly called *toothpicks,*" said one writer, in 1708, though we can be sure that a toothpick by any other name would be just as vulgar.

Scalpere is the parent also of the Latin *scalprum,* knife, and *scalpellum,* little knife. The word *scalpel* derives from this diminuitive, *scalpellum.*

(The word *scalp,* noun and verb, comes from a different family — from a Scandinavian word meaning shell, or *scallop.* It must be admitted, however, that the American Indian did much to relate *scalp* to the knife. Not to mention that notorious skinner, the ticket-scalper.)

ʹZʹ

(and why it was sent to the rrrrear of the alphabet)

In *King Lear,* the Earl of Kent rages at Oswald. "Thou whoreson *zed!* Thou unnecessary letter!"

While the comparison was hardly complimentary, none can deny its plausibility. The *z,* or *zed* as the English call it, was indeed at one time an "unnecessary letter."*

The Earl, however, was showing the traditional disregard for the horse turned out to pasture. The *z* hadn't always been unnecessary. It once occupied the No. 7 spot in the Roman alphabet, and might still occupy a front position it if hadn't contracted a bad case of rhotacism.

Rhotacism (from *rho,* the Greek name for *r*) is the tendency of the human tongue in some languages to trill or "roll" the *r*-sound. Immune to it as English-speakers are, it is difficult for some of us to understand how this roll of the *r* can terminate with a sound like *sssss* and the softer *zzzzzz.* But that it can. And did. The example most often held up is the Latin *flos,* pronounced with a soft ending, "floze." This is the ancestor of *flora* and *floral,* which today might be "flosa" and "flosal" if rhotacism hadn't interfered. With the *r* so potently delivering the *z*-sound, the early Romans simply kicked the *z* out of the alphabet and let the *r* do its work.

Later, during the time of Cicero, when many Greek words were being adopted by Latin, the *z* was needed again. And so it was resurrected, and once again became a part of the alphabet. The comeback, however, was somewhat less than triumphant. The *z*

---

*You've heard the expression, "from A to Izzard." *Izzard* was another English name for the letter *z,* as were *ezod, uzzard* and *zad.*

wasn't restored to its old spot in the sun, but rather tacked on at the very end, doomed probably for the rest of its life to be an alphabetical caboose.

'razz'

('razzberry' is just the half of it)

"Razz" is short for "razzberry," that derisive blurt known also as "the Bronx cheer."

It derives from an interesting rhyming slang believed to have originated with the street vendors, beggars, and thieves of London's Cockney demi-monde, in the late 1880s.

A nonsensical thing, as most speech fads are,* this slang, is built on two- and three-word phrases whose final word always rhymes with the legitimate word being "slanged." For example, a *bed* is an *Uncle Ned*, and a *table* is a *Cain and Abel*. *Money* is *bees and honey, eyes* is *mince pies,* and *fist* is *Oliver Twist. Tea* is *Rosy* (or *Betty) Lee, whore* is *forty-four,* piano is *Old Joanna, bird* is *Richard the Third, jail* is *moan and wail, limousine* is *seldom seen, whisky* is *gay and frisky, girl* is *twist and twirl,* and *neck* is *Gregory Peck.*

If an elephant's trunk got soaked in the France and Spain, his trouble and strife might stand him in front of the Anna Maria and give him a bull and cow. This translates into, "If a drunk got soaked in the rain, his wife might stand him in front of the fire and give him a row."

Sometimes the original two- or three-word term was shortened to just the initial word. For instance, "I put my loaf on the weeping to catch a spot of bo." Here *loaf* is short for *loaf of bread* (head), while *weeping* is *weeping willow* (pillow), and *bo* is for

---

*In the United States, not many years ago, there was a brief vogue for a rhyming slang typified by "cruisin' for a bruisin,'" "achin' for a breakin,'" etc. "Double talk" is another such fad. "Back slang," *yob* for *boy, elrig* for *girl,"* goes back as far as "center slang" which, as every schoolboy knows, is igPay atin Lay.

Bo-Peep (sleep). Thus: "I put my head on the pillow to catch a spot of sleep."

The familiar expression, *brass tacks,* although assigned various other origins by folk etymology, actually is rhyming slang for *facts.* To get down to brass tacks was, and still is, to get down to facts.

As for *razzberry,* it's just half of the two-word term that originally named the Bronx cheer. The other half, long since dropped off, was *tart.* A *razzberry-tart* was rhyming slang for that which you probably can guess, and which, if you can't, this book will never tell you.

'Greece'

(the Italians had a word for it)

The Latin word *uitulus* meant "calf." This is the origin of *Uitalia,* the name of a land which, in ancient times, was great cow country. Later the initial *U* was claimed by aphesis, leaving the present-day *Italia* and its English equivalent, *Italy.* (The Greeks borrowed the word *uitalis,* incidentally, and converted it into *italos,* their word for "bull").

The name *Greece* also came from the Latin language. The Greeks called themselves Hellenes, from the name of their legendary ancestor, Hellen. The tribe of Hellenes who lived in the west, nearest to Italy, were called *Graikoi.* The Italians latinized *Graikoi* to *Graecus,* plural *Graeci,* and then, applying the tribal name to Hellenes as a whole, named their land *Graecia.* The English *Greece* followed, along with visibly related names in virtually all Germanic and Romance languages.

'coward'

(and why Noel isn't unhappy with his name)

The adjective *caudal,* as in *caudal fin,* "tail fin," is formed from the Latin word *cauda,* meaning tail. *Cauda* produced a variant form, *coda,* which went into Old French as *coe.*

This was the beginning of the Old French *couard*, "coward," figuratively one with his tail between his legs, one who turns tail. The suffix *-ard* (see *'bastard*) commonly denotes a discreditable excess, as in *drunkard, sluggard, dullard, niggard*, etc. A coward, to his discredit, is excessively afraid.

Someone once suggested that Noel Coward should change his name. On the surface, this seems reasonable. *Coward* isn't exactly a name to get elected to Congress with. But the *noun* coward and the *surname* Coward are two different things. Noel Coward lives quite content with his name, knowing that it has nothing to do with cowardice. It's a surname of the Occupational Class, the tongue's alteration of *cowherd*, and therefore no more defamatory than *Shepherd* for *sheepherd* or *Eward* for *ewe-herd*.

And anyway, cowards are not always cowardly when the chips are down. As R. B. Barham pointed out:

"Cowards, 'tis said, in certain situations,
    Derive a sort of courage from despair,
And then perform, from downright desperation,
    Much more than a bolder man would dare."

It's the old story of the cornered rat; pick on him if need be, but always give him enough room to escape.

'curfew'

(a medieval cover-up)

The popular meaning of *curfew*, today, is "time to get the kids off the street."

During the Middle Ages, *curfew* called for a different kind of nocturnal precaution.

People lived perpetually in fear of fire.

Houses were highly inflammable. Just one little spark, sometimes, and — *whoosh* — hot time in the old town tonight.

Accordingly, most villages had a village bell which was rung at bedtime, to remind the people to cover their fires before turning in. If there was no village bell, a man sometimes went through the lanes with a hand-bell.

In France and Norman England, the name of this early warning system was *couvre feu,* "to cover the fire." By elision* this name became "cur'feu," which subsequently was spelled as we know it today, *curfew.*

This same mutation gave us the word *kerchief,* from the French *couvre chef,* meaning "cover the head," or head-cover. Today, *chef* designates a "head-person", a *chief,* but at the time it was a running mate of the medieval French *teste,* whence *tete,* a reference to the head of the body.

It wouldn't hurt if curfew got some of the grown-ups off the street, too.

'gardyloo'

(also *bed-swerver, dilling, anywhen,*
and other memorable has-beens from
the days when one woman was a whole *brothel*)

"She had made the gardyloo out the wrong window," wrote Sir Walter Scott. *Gardyloo* is a souvenir of those ante-plumbing times when waste water was disposed of by tossing it out the nearest window. As fair warning to passers-by, the tosser before tossing cried out "Gardyloo!", a corruption of the French "Gardez de l'eau," meaning "Watch out for the water."

Gardyloo is one of a host of once-common words and expressions which have retired from the active English language. But which, like any other charming curiosity, deserve occasionally to be offered for public enjoyment.

---

*Elision is the omission or slurring-over of a syllable in pronunciation. Although usually involuntary in speech, it is both deliberate and helpful in the writing of poetry, *o'er* and *e'er* being well-worn examples, along with *'tis,* which is an elided coalescence. Everybody who ever said "ever'body" has made use of elision. So has everybody who ever said "everybody," for that matter; the word *every* is itself the elision of "ever each."

Ninnybroth, for example, was coffee, at that time when some Englishmen felt that only an *innocent,* a gull or simpleton, would drink it. *Ninny,* a word still in use, was a slangy coalescence of *an innocent* to an *"inny,"* which then by metanalysis became *a ninny* (see *'nickname').*

A *bed-swerver* was an unfaithful wife and a *deywife* was a dairy-wife, i.e., dairy-woman, milkmaid.

To *kittle* someone was to tickle him, a word no odder than *tickle,* when one thinks about it.

Calliblephary was an eye-lid coloring, from the Greek *kallos,* beauty + *blepharon,* eye-lid. "The marrow of the right fore legge with soot . . . serveth for a calliblephary," wrote Robert Lovell in *A Compleat History of Animals and Minerals* (1661).

Affodil was the name of asphodel, that narcissus-like flower we know today as *daffodil,* and *affy* meant to trust or entrust, hence the present-day word *affiance.* If *affy* seems odd, remember our own *defy.* Idols or false gods were *afgods,* "off-gods," from the Old English *af,* "off."

Bouk meant belly, and *bouksome* meant paunchy, or big-bellied. The word is related to the one which produced *Buick,* a surname of Dutch origin meaning "big-bellied." (The similarity of *bouksome* to *buxom* is coincidental).

A *dilling,* possibly corrupted from *darling,* was a child born to parents who were past the age when parents usually have children. To *cose* was to make cozy, and *barbery* was that institution we know today as a barber shop.

A *ballard* was a bald-headed man, a *dizzard* was a fool, and a *dolk* was a dimple, while *dout* meant "do out," just as *doff* means "do off" and *don* means "do on."

Brothel at first meant any worthless person, from *brothen,* "to go to ruin." Later it came to mean a worthless woman, then a prostitute. The term *brothel's house* was shortened to *brothel,* which thus came to represent the establishment rather than the personal purveyor of its wares.

That phenomenon we know today as *hindsight* was earlier called *afterwit*. A *crack-halter* was a predestinate gallows-bird, i.e., one who would one day *crack* (tauten) the *halter* (rope). *Crackrope* also was used.

An *amober* was a "maiden fee," that established sum for which a bridegroom might rescue his bride from *prima noctis,* the right of the Welsh lord to spend the first night with the new wife. In France, the equivalent privilege of "first night" was called *droit du seigneur.*

Evite was the word for a scantily-dressed woman, constructed jocularly from *Eve.* Addison in *The Guardian,* 1713, reported that "the Evites daily increase," and predicted that "fig-leaves are shortly coming into fashion." O, Addison, that thou should have lived to see this day!

A homosexual was a *badling. Epicene,* a noun referring to one with the characteristics of both sexes, was by extension an adjective meaning effeminate. *Old,* which has only one meaning today, once had several contingent connotations, e.g., *abundant,* from the sense of long continuity, and *skilled,* from that of long experience. "The Germans were too *old* for us there," wrote Daniel Defoe in *Colonel Jack.*

Monthly was used for *madly,* i.e., lunatic or "moon-touched," and a *moonling* was a fool (see' *-ling').*

Yesternight was the teammate of *yesterday. Yestreen* was an elided coalescence of *yester-evening,* and "day before yesterday" was represented by *hereyesterday,* probably a corruption of *ere-yesterday.*

> *Anywhen* meant just what you'd guess, "anytime," and *elsewhen* meant "at some other time," just as *elsewhere* today means "at some other place." *Somewhen,* "sometime," and *somewhither,* "somewhere," were used, as was *anywhither,* "anywhere."

Himpnes was a variant form of *hymns.* A *frowze* was a ladies' wig, and *foumart,* from "foul marten," was another name for the polecat (see *'polecat'*). A *lungis* was a long, lanky, lazy fellow, or, as defined by Minsheu in 1617, "a slimme slowback, a dreaming gangril, a tall and dull slangam." *Lungis* is related to the present-day word *lounge.*

Panse was an old equivalent of *think,* from the French *penser,* and a *coverslut* was a kimono or wrapper, the term *slut* referring not to the wearer's morals but to her personal slovenliness.

Thomas De Quincy, some years after he confessed to drinking a quart of "ruby-red laudanum" every night, claimed to have coined the word *infibulate,* having never seen it before. This is quite possible, for men, being men, frequently arrive at identical ideas at different times and places. Be that as it may, *infibulate* was listed much earlier in dictionaries. It meant "to fix," a special kind of *fixing* or *fastening,* from the Latin *in* + *fibula,* "fastening" – in this case the fastening of a chastity belt on females. Also, as indicated by John Bulwer in 1650, "the buttoning-up of the prepuce" of young Roman male singers "with a brass or silver button."

A *parnel* or *pernel* was a priest's mistress, ultimately from the Latin *Petronilla,* feminine diminuitive of *Peter,* i.e., "Peter's woman." A *posy* was a short motto, and *pardee* was a mild oath, a euphemism of the French *par Dieu,* "by God," roughly the same as "by golly."

A *hiren* was a siren, seductive woman, for hire, and after folk etymology created the term *helpmate* from the Biblical "an help meet for him," there understandably followed its now oboslete opposite, *hindermate.*

Prickmedaintie defined anyone, male or female, who was over-finicky about personal appearance. *Shunless* was "unavoidable." *Tind* meant to kindle, a form related to *tinder,* and an *arming* was any wretched creation, from the Old English *earm,* poor.

Wowe was an early form of *woo,* and pronounced just that way, "woo." Speaking of which, anyone familiar with the pet obsession of that lovable delinquent, Samuel Pepys, will know what he was referring to when he wrote in his *Diary* (December 18, 1661) that he'd gone to church and there "spent most of my time looking on my new morena." A *morena* was a brunette. The word probably was related to *Moor,* along with *morella,* dark cloth, and *morello,* dark red cherry. Blondes and redheads should not infer that Samuel had any pronounced preference for brunettes. He was entirely too preoccupied with those features women have in common, ever to have been prejudiced by their trivial differences.

'transliteration'

(The Midnight Ride of *Whom?*)

Wistinghausen became *Westinghouse* and William *Sonntag* turned out to be Billy *Sunday*. Men are migratory creatures, and when they take up homes in new lands, they like to blend in. In many cases, one of the first things they do is get rid of odd-sounding, foreign-looking names.

Translation is one simple way of doing this. The Czech *Kovar* translates to the American *Smith,* as do the Irish *Gowan* and *McGowan.* Monsieur *Poulain,* by translation, becomes Mr. *Colt.* The German name *Geiger* becomes *Fiddler,* and the Polish *Zurek* and Italian *Zola* both translate into *Hill.*

The other common means of changing a name without scrapping all connection with the past is called *transliteration.* While translation changes the sound without changing the meaning, *transliteration* surrenders the meaning but hangs on to the sound. For example, in the novel, *Hilda Lessways,* Arnold Bennett wrote of "a French modeller named Canonges who had officially changed the name to Cannon because no one in the five towns could pronounce it correctly."

There was a man from the Isle of Guernsey who had a similar problem. He lived in Boston. His name was Apollos Rivoire, but nobody could pronounce it right, so he changed it. If he hadn't, Longfellow would have had to call his poem *The Midnight Ride of Apollos Rivoire, Jr.*

'none'

(also two *no's* and a *nay*)

There are two *no's* in the English language.

The first is an adverb, as in the expression, "No, no, a thousand times, no." Its story begins, really, with the Old English *a,* Middle English *ai,* both meaning "always, ever." (This is the same *a, ai* that evolved into the word *aye,* whose original meaning of "ever", as in the expression, "forever and aye," later shifted somewhat to that of an affirmative).

The opposite of *a*, ever, was *na*, never. This *na* subsequently took a softer pronunciation, and along with it the spelling that converted it into the modern adverb *no*. (The same process, incidentally, turned the Middle English *ai* into *nay*).

The other *no* is an adjective, as in "no man's land," "no time like the present," etc. This *no*, very simply, is a shortened form of the pronoun *none*.

None began as the Old English *nan*, a compound of *ne*, not + *an*, one. In the early English period *nan* became *non*, later picking up the terminal *e* for the present-day spelling, *none*, which still retains the original meaning, "no one" or "not one."

If you believe it's correct to say "none *is*" and incorrect to say "none *are*," many will agree with you. The late and deservedly great Professor William Strunk, Jr., made no bones about it in his *The Elements of Style: "None*. Takes the singular verb."

On the other hand, the late and deservedly great H. W. Fowler of Oxford, in his *Dictionary of Modern English Usage*, said: "It is a mistake to suppose that the pronoun *(none)* is singular only."

Oh, well, none of us are perfect, are he? The important thing to recognize is that when a majority of people say "None are," for a long-enough time, it will become correct. One might as easily clean the Augean stables as impede the pronunciation, spelling, meaning, or grammatical conduct of a word in whatever direction popular usage decides it shall take. Obedient to the logic that *none* means "not *one*," I confess to a prejudice in favor of Dr. Strunk's viewpoint. But this is a personal bullheadedness which will be to no avail. Popular usage wears no logic's collar. It is like Humpty-Dumpty, who said, "When I use a word, it means what I want it to mean."

'quick'

(which fingernails are bitten to)

The word *quick*, originally, had nothing to do with speed. It meant "alive." An expectant mother who could feel her unborn child stirring within her body, for example, was said to be "quick with child."

This meaning is still implicit in words such as *quicksand* and *quicksilver*. To bite fingernails "to the quick" is to chew them down to the *live* flesh. A remark that "cuts to the quick" cuts figuratively to the sensitive, or living, flesh. *Quick-fence* was once the name for a fence of living shrubbery, *quickstock* was the forerunner of the present-day *livestock*, and Shakespeare wrote of a medicine powerful enough "to quicken a rocke."

In this earlier sense, *quick* probably is best known today for its place in the King James Bible passage, "the judge of quick and dead," *Acts 10:42*. A passage from *Ephesians*, which in the King James reads "hath *quickened* us together with Christ," has in the Revised Standard version been updated to "hath made us *alive* together with Christ."

The word derives from the Germanic, where it's seen as the Old High German *queck*, Old Saxon *quik*, Old English *cwic*, Swedish *qvick* and Danish *kvik*.

How did *quick*, "alive," give us *quick*, "speedy?" The same way *live* gave us *lively*, if you'll permit a quick answer.

'grocer'

(man known for his spicy utterings)

In England four hundred years ago, that retailer now known as a *grocer* was strictly a wholesaler.

The Middle English *grosser* was a borrowing of the French *grossier*, itself an extension of the Old French *gros*, meaning large, bulky. Thus the meaning, one who sold in bulk, by the large or *whole* lot, or, as we sometimes say today, by the *gross*.

In those days, the grocer's wares were sugar and spices imported from the East. These commodities, in fact, were so closely identified with him that the captain of an East Indiaman was known as a "grosser captain," and that occupational eczema caused by handling sugar was called "grocer's itch."

The word *grossery* had not yet come to mean a place where "grosseries" were bought. Dictionaries of the times defined it as "the uttering of wares by wholesale." This is a definition which may itself bear a little defining:

Today, we relate the word *utter* to speech, but originally it had a much broader meaning. It derives from the Old English *utian,* meaning "to *out* with," or as we'd say today, "to *come out* with." This sense is retained when something new on the market is said to be "Just out!" or when Detroit "comes out" with its new auto designs, or when some manufacturer is said to "bring out" a new whatsis or "put out" the best whatsis on the market. *Out,* of course, is also related to speech, as when we invite someone who has something on his chest, "All right, out with it!"

The modern word *out* is a derivative of *ut,* from the Old English *utian.* The identity survives today in words such as *utmost,* "outmost," and *utterly,* "to outer extremes."

'retailer'

(a cutter-upper)

A retailer sells in small lots, or *pieces* of the whole-sale. He sells "*piece*-meal."

This meaning of "pieces" is explicit in the main element of the word *retailer.* It derives from the Old Franch *tailleur,* "to cut to pieces."

Tailor, a "cutter," is visibly related to *retailer.*

So is *detail,* the details being the little pieces that make up the whole.

And so is *tally,* meaning to keep score. This meaning came from the ancient custom of *cutting* notches on sticks to keep records, and there's an interesting little story that goes with it:

In England's Exchequer during the 17th century, two strips of wood, or tallies, were laid face-to-face and notched simultaneously, on their edges, to indicate that a deposit had been made. The Exchequer retained one of the tallies; the depositor took the other. When a withdrawal was made, the notches on the tallies had to match, or "tally." The system became obsolete in 1826, and after eight years the Exchequer decided to dispose of the mountains of tallies that were still stored away. This marked the passing of a tradition, the end of an era, and it was decided that a ceremony was in order. The tallies were collected and piled high for a proper ceremonial bonfire, which, when lit, most unceremoniously burnt to the ground the Palace of Westminster and both Houses of Parliament.

'sincere'

(you could be sure it was pure)

If you write a letter to a friend and close it, *Yours, without wax,* he'll probably think you've been out in the sun too long.

Actually, though, you'd only be using the original and literal meaning of *Yours, sincerely.*

Begin with the *sin* in *sincere.* It's from the Latin *sine,* meaning "without". You see it in *sinecure,* a job that pays a salary without work, and in the term *sine die,* which describes a meeting adjourned without a date for the next meeting.

Now, take the other half of sincere, *cere.* It comes from the Latin *cera* and means "wax" (and is kin, incidentally, to the Greek *keros,* which gave us *kerosene*).

You see *cera* in *cerecloth,* the fabric doused in melted wax to make a shroud. Shakespeare used it when Hamlet asked his father's ghost, "Why thy canonized bones, hearsed in death, have burst their *cerements?"*

Sincere, therefore, means *without wax.*

But why this odd expression?

Some authorities say deceitful potters used to fill pottery cracks with wax to fool buyers. Sincere pottery, then, was pottery without wax.

Others say it was a term invented specifically to describe honey that had no wax in it.

Honey without wax was pure honey, and so sincere has come to mean pure, true, honest.

Here's hoping your honey is sincere.

'mama'

(and a matter of embarrassment to papas)

The golden word *mama,* or something very close to it, can be found in virtually all languages. Among the Indo-European family, there's the Sanskrit *ma,* Latin *mamma,* Greek *mamma,* Albanian *ama,* French *maman,* Russian *mama,* Assyrian *ummu,* Dutch *mama,* Welsh *mam,* Italian *mamma,* Spanish *mama,* etc., etc., etc.

But in no case is *mama* to be considered as a product of the Indo-European or any other language family. It's not a learned word. It's an instinctive human utterance. It's the spontaneous sound the baby makes when he cries for his mother's breast, and it occurs just as readily in Swahili or Bantu or Japanese as in any other language.

Bear in mind that this is not a cry for the *mother*. Not at first. It's a cry for food, at a time when the baby doesn't realize that *he* exists, much less his mother. Gradually he understands that this warm thing who takes him up in her arms is his meal ticket, and that this sound he made accidentally, if made on purpose, will make the warm thing come running.

Since he chooses to call her "ma-ma," grown-ups go along with him and *name* her Mama. But *only* because he calls her that. If for any reason this first human utterance should change, to *lala* or *bobo* for instance, the word *mama* will disappear and mamas the world over will be known as lalas or bobos.

As a matter of physiology, this is most unlikely. The baby makes the "mama" sound first because the labial muscles that produce this sound are the first that are ready to be used. Ready because they're the same muscles he exercises in getting his food.

The Greenlandic verb *amama* means "to suckle." The Latin *mamma*, also meaning "breast," gave us such words as *mammary* and *mammal*. Eric Partridge suggests that the basic *ma-ma* sound may be represented even in the Egyptian *mest-t* and the Australian aboriginal *namma*, "breast."

Now get ready for a shock, men.

It seems that the sound of *p* also requires very little labial effort. *Papa*, therefore, also is an instinctive infantile cry for food, running *mama* a poor but undeniable second. In fact, *papa* led to *pap*, meaning baby food, and to *papillary*, which pertains to the nipples. Just where this leaves us papas is debatable, and it is best not to discuss it further.

'by'

(such a little word for so many meanings)

The word *by* has numerous meanings, or numerous shades of the same meaning, and we grow up using the whole assortment without ever realizing what a range of important little differences it puts at our command. For example, it means:

> *near to* and *alongside,* as in "down *by* the riverside"
> *of* or *from,* as in *"by* Pearl S. Buck"
> *toward,* as in "north *by* northwest"
> *past,* as in "the caissons go rolling *by"*
> *according to,* as in *"by* the clock"
> *not later than,* as in "Be ready *by* noon"
> *by means of,* as in *"by* dawn's early light"
> *with respect to,* as in "He did well *by* his family"
> *sanction,* or *witness,* as in "By the Almighty!"
> *aside,* as in *"By the way";* also as in *"by* the *by,"*
> in which the second *by* stands for "side," as suggest-
> ed by *by*-way and *by*-road, "side road."

By came into Old English as *bi,* directly from the Old High German *bi* — which was a shortening of *umbi,* a primitive Germanic word related to the Latin *ambi,* Sanskrit *abhi,* and Greek *amphi.* All these ancient words meant "around, alongside, about," and they're seen in such modern English words as *ambitious,* "a going about"; *ambiguous,* "roundabout," and *amphitheatre,* a "stage with sides all around."

But most interesting of all, perhaps, is the way *by* disguises itself in our multitude of "be"-words. *Belief,* for example, literally means "by-live," i.e., something to live by. And *because* means "by cause of."

Used as a separate word, the Old English spelling *bi* prevailed, as in "bi god." But in composition with other words, it usually took the form *be.* We all know that *beside* really means "by(the)side," a significance sustained also in *beneath, behind, before, below, betwixt* and *between (by the twain).*

This *be* is sometimes used to intensify words and sometimes to indicate cause, as in *befriend, bedeck, behead, begrudge, belabor, bewitch, befuddle, bereave, bedraggle, beguile, bewilder, becalm, belittle, berate,* and many, many others. Including *beseech.* This particular word derives from the Old English *secan,* Middle English *secen,* which meant "to seek, to search out." And which explains why we tell dogs to "sic 'em," by the by.

'noise'

(a sickening story)

The word *noise* looks and sounds much like the Greek word *naus*, so there's nothing very surprising about the fact that it derives from *naus*.

The surprising thing is that *naus* didn't mean *noise*. It meant *ship*. You can see it in the word *nautical*, in the name *Argonaut*, and in the title of Holmes' *The Chambered Nautilus*, a poem about the shellfish which is reputed to have a membrane it can set like a sail.

The Latin language borrowed *naus* from the Greek. It retained the meaning, "ship," but having no *u* in its alphabet, represented the word as *navs* (see *'manuscript u'*). *Navs* became the later Latin form *navis*, and thus led to such words as *navy* and *navigate*.

But none of this explains why the English word *noise* came from the Greek word for *ship*. Were the Greek ships noisy?

No, the Greek ships weren't noisy.

Just the Greek passengers.

Which is better understood when we know that *nausea* is another word we obtained from *naus*. Today, *nausea* means any dizzy, where's-the-nearest-potty feeling, but originally it applied only to seasickness. Or, as it was known then, *ship-sickness*. Anybody who has ever found himself with a boatload of seasick passengers knows that things can get pretty noisy. Remember this little story, in case you see a seasick passenger who needs cheering up. It'll give him an upchuckle.

'pregnant'

(it's full of promise)

The *g* dropped away from the old Latin word *gnatus*. This left *natus*, meaning "one who is born."

Natus is the immediate origin of *native*.

Natal, *nascent*, and *innate* also are closely related to *natus*, as are the names *Natalie*, *Natalia*, and *Natasha*, which mean "birthday," with specific reference to the birth of Jesus, *The Nativity*.

But we also have from *gnatus* a few words which held on to the g. For example, the little-known *agnate*, something born in addition to; the better-known *cognate*, something co-born or born along with, and the exceedingly well-known *pregnant*, which refers to something "pre-borning" or not yet born but promising to be.

Pregnant, therefore, is not restricted to the meaning, "big with child." It describes anything that is big with promise. A pregnant remark is one full of sub-surface meaning which promises later to be borne out. And pregnancy, of course, is a com*promising* situation. Especially when without benefit of clergy. As it is writ, the only thing more revealing than a maternity dress is a paternity suit.

'testicle'

(from an ancient word meaning *three*)

The Indo-European word for "three" was *trei.*

It was the starting point for *triangle, trinity, trivial,* and many other words which depend upon that invaluable little prefix, *tri-.*

It also was the starting point for the name of that invaluable little affix upon which the human race depends, the *testicle.*

Granted that the testicle is more commonly regarded as part of a twosome, the concept of *three* is easily understandable. But as a preliminary, consider several other words:

The word *trivial,* for example. This is a compound of *tri + via,* or "three" + "way." It was a reference to that point at which one road forks into two other roads, the junction of three *ways.* In ancient times such junctions, like today's rural crossroads store, were natural meeting-places for people. Here they traded gossip, boasted, and engaged in general small talk which was so little to be taken seriously that it prompted the description *trivial.* This word, referring originally to what we know today as "scuttlebutt," gradually came to signify anything of little importance, anything *trifling.*

Trio comes from *trei* through Latin and Italian, while such words as *treble, trellis, trefoil* and *trey* (as in *trey of spades*) have the same origin through Latin and French.

Travel, interestingly, also derives ultimately from the

Indo-European *trei*. The Roman tripalium (*tri* + *palus*, "paling, stake") was a torture machine with three sharp-pointed stakes. It led to the Vulgar Latin verb *tripaliare*, meaning to torture. In Old French, *tripaliare* became *traveillier*, from which there came the noun *travail*, meaning any agonizing labor. Including journeying, which in ancient times was a tortuous ordeal. *Travail* thus became the forerunner of the present-day word *travel*.

Now, *testicle:*

The Indo-European *trei* had the variant form, *ter.* It contributed the meaning of "three" to such Latin-sprung words as *tercentenary, tertiary* and *tierce.*

In this mother-tongue, *sti* was a variant of *sta*, "stand." *Stis* signified one who stood, a stander.

These two words, *ter* + *stis*, became *terstis.* Literally, this compound meant "third-stander." Figuratively, it meant "bystander," as when a third person stood by and listened to two others who were agreeing or disagreeing, or making a bargain with each other. In this sense, the concept of "bystander" or "third-stander" was that of a *witness,* and *terstis* through Latin became the origin of such words as *testament, attest, testify, testimony.*

And therein lies the connection of *trei* to *testicle.* The word *testicles* is a diminuitive of *testes,* with the literal meaning of "little testifiers." Testifiers to a man's virility, perhaps, much as the vulgar "He's got *balls"* is a modern testimonial to male-power. But more likely, known as testifiers because of an old and widespread custom men once had, that of taking an oath or swearing by what they considered their most precious endowments. Any etymology suggesting that these by-standers were so named because, in time of need, they stood by a man, is folk etymology. But ingenious.

'preternatural'

(Doin' what comes naturally — but not yet)

Until the 15th century, there was good reason to believe that a ship could sail right off the edge of the world.

There was also good reason to believe that it *couldn't*, but men didn't know the reason at the time. As soon as they found it out, it became ridiculously obvious.

But then another puzzlesome question arose:

How could ships and people and things in general stick to the sides and bottom of a globe?

Apples had fallen from trees for eons, but Sir Isaac Newton had to get hit over the head before he discovered the answer to that one. As soon as he discovered it, it also became instantly obvious.

The word for this sort of thing is *preternatural,* meaning something that's perfectly understandable, but not just yet. It's one of numerous words, such as *preterist, preterablent, pretermit,* and *preterite,* all built upon the Latin adverb and preposition *praeter,* meaning a going-past, a going-beyond, a transcending.

When I was a tad, there was a little girl on Vineyard Street who was a very pretty little girl. She had long, golden hair way down past her shoulders. Little boys were forever trying to kiss her. It was quite a problem. She couldn't go outdoors without getting kissed. Finally, her mother told her how to solve the problem. After that, when she went outdoors and a little boy lunged for her, she'd just stick out her tongue, and the little boy would come to a screeching halt.

This, it should be pointed out, is a defense that will work only on very little boys. Kissing, like time, marches on. In the meantime, if you have a little girl who hates to get kissed, and wonders why people do it, tell her it's preternatural. Perfectly understandable — but not just yet.

'aunt,' 'ain't,' 'ant'

(three words that ran into the same snag)

As every saltworthy crossword puzzle-worker knows, an *emmet* is an ant.

Emmet comes from the Old English *aemette,* a derivative of the Germanic *ameise,* meaning "to cut off." Ants are accomplished cutters, or gnawers.

Thanks to elision, *aemette* became *aemtte,* or *amte.*

In this form, *amte,* it immediately ran into a notorious phonetic snag — the difficulty of pronouncing the sound of *mt* without intruding the sound of *p. Amte* simply comes out "ampte."

There were two ways to deal with such a problem:

1. Admit the *p* and go about your business. That's how the *p* arrived in the word *empty*, from the Old English *emtig, aemtig*. It also accounts for the appearance of the *p* in the place-name *Ampthill*.

2. Let nature take its course. In that case, the *m*-sound would turn to the *n*-sound, as it almost always does when followed by the *t*-sound. This is the phonetic law that produced *identical*, instead of *idemtical*, from the Latin *idem*.

By letting nature take its course, *amte* became *ante*. After which, the terminal *e* dropped away, as it has from manye olde wordes, and *ante* became *ant*.

Now, please consider the word *aunt*, which comes as an Anglo-Norman development, *aunte*, from the Latin *amita*.

At first, *amita* was pronounced "ahm-ee-tuh," but here also elision removed the middle syllable, leaving the pronunciation "ahm-tuh." This brought up that same old trouble-maker, *m* before *t*. Again the law applied, and the result was "ahn-tuh," *aunte*, which time polished to *"ahnt," aunt*.

Finally, the word *ain't*. It's a contraction, of course, of *am not*, a colloquialism which properly should be *amn't*. But that's a tongue-twister. Something had to go. Any attempt to drop the *n*-sound left the troublesome *m-before-t* snag, and brought the *n* hurrying back. As a result, *amn't* became *ant*, later softening to *ain't*.

There is one possible benefit from reading all this. It will fortify anyone who wants to bet that the correct pronunciation of *aunt* is "ahnt," not "ant." *Aunt* ain't "ant."

'liefer'

(or, if you'd rather, *rather*)

Liefer, sometimes *lever*, is an archaic word meaning "sooner," or "rather." It's from the Old English *leof*, meaning "pleasing." To say "I'd liefer sleep than get up" is to profess a greater pleasure from sleeping than from arising.

Liefer is as dead as a doornail, but *lief* hasn't yet been totally abandoned. "I'd as lief," meaning "I'd as soon," is still heard occasionally, depending on the company one keeps.

'rather'

(also *rathe, rathely* and *ratherest*)

The Old English *hraeth* meant "quick, speedy."

It was the precursor of the now obsolete *rathe*, which meant "early, soon."

Rathe was common in the 14th and 15th centuries. Milton wrote of "the rathe primrose," and Michael Drayton referred to "the rathe morning."

From this adjective, *rathe*, there came an adverb, *rathely*. It meant "earlily, promptly, firstly."

This sense of earlyness or soon-ness led also to the adverb *rather*. At first it meant "sooner," and the connotation of precedence in time gradually became one of preference by choice, e.g., "Mother, I'd *rather* do it myself!" The expression, "I'd sooner," is still quite common for "I'd rather."

After *rather*, the comparative degree of *rathe*, there came *ratherest*, its superlative form.

Rathe, rathely and *ratherest* are lost and by the wind grieved, but *rather* is still going great guns. It has a *rather* promising future — and in *that* usage, brings up another meaning of *rather* which is rather too much to tackle at the moment.

'manure'

(at first, no reason to turn up the nose)

Main is French for hand, and *oeuvre* is French for work. Put together, these words form the compound *manoeuvre* (English *maneuver*) which originally meant "hand-work," or manual labor.

They also demonstrate the origin of the word *manure*, a shortening of *manoeuvre*, which at first meant nothing more revolting than "farming by hand." This meaning of hand-tillage is exemplified in Bacon's history of the reign of Henry VII — "Arable land which could not be *manured* without people or families was turned into pasture." Also in Milton's *Reason of Church Government*: "The *manuring* hand of the tiller shall root up all that burdens the soil."

But along the way, probably before the original meaning had fully died out, *manure* picked up its present-day meaning. The fertilizer sense is unmistakable in *Othello*, when Iago says, "Either to have it sterile with idleness or manured with industry."

In addition to *manure*, the French *oeuvre*, work, has made the same contribution to such words as litera*ture*, a work of letters; scrip*ture*, a work of writing; furni*ture*, a work of furnishing; cul*ture*, a work of cultivation, etc.

The word *manure*, it seems, suffers somewhat like Julius Caesar. The good things about it are forgotten, but the bad live on.

'Jamestown'

(Master Carlton would spin in his grave)

The settlers of the first permanent English colony in America named it *James-town*, and this displeased Master Dudley Carlton.

Master Carlton was a professor at Oxford. He belonged to a clique of educated Englishmen who liked to hoot and sneer at the place-names the American colonists were inventing and/or adopting from the Indians.

Of *James-town*, he wrote, "Methinks the town hath no graceful name." Later he wrote, "Master Warner has a letter from Master George Percy who names their town *James-fort*, which we like best of all because it comes near to *Chemesford*."

Ah-ha.

What Master Carlton and his fellow Masters really wanted for the Colonies was second-hand names imported from England. They liked *James-fort* because it sounded like *Chemesford*, the name of the English town which once had been *Chemesfort* and which now is *Chelmsford*. Both "Chemes" and "Chelms" were mouthings of the name of the English sovereign, James I, mouthed as only the English could mouth it.

Some of the Jamestown settlers also preferred the name

James-fort, and that's what it might be today if the others hadn't put up such a stiff opposition. An opposition still audible in the way we pronounce *Jamestown,* incidentally. Whereas many *towns* have turned to *tons* — Bos*ton,* New*ton,* Prince*ton,* Kings*ton,* etc. — that unbudging fight for *-town* started *Jamestown* off with an emphasis that's just as unmistakable today as it was 350 years ago.

If a little thing like *Jamestown* upset Master Carlton, think how he'd spin in his grave if he knew that right there in the state named for his Virgin Queen, Virginians went on to memorialize such place-names as Cash, Check, Cripple Creek, Harryhogan, Horsepen, Keezletown, Hustle, Overall and Teetotum. Not to mention Bumpass.

'gingerly'

(proving that everybody makes mistakes)

The word *gingerly,* of course, has nothing to do with ginger. It means "cautiously". But it implies a specialized kind of caution, one born more of obedience than of will; a soft, quiet obeisance converted by fear into a hair-trigger readiness to bolt and run.

Fowler's *Modern English Usage,* frequently as delightful to enjoy as it is helpful to use, says *gingerly* has the same meaning the Bible translators had in mind when they used *delicately* to describe how Agag obeyed Samuel's summons to come and be chopped to pieces.

The word apparently derives from the Old French *gensor, genzor,* a comparative form of the Old French *gent,* Latin *genitum,* meaning well-born, genteel, gentle. Fowler says Skeats connects it with the Old English *gang,* "going". What this proves is that even the great can make mistakes. Not the great Skeats, in this case, but the great Fowler. Or perhaps the great Sir Ernest Gowers who has revised and edited the great Fowler. For Skeats makes no such connection; in fact, he offers the etymology given above, adding that *gent* was also used as a positive in the sense of "pretty, delicate".

Gingerly is a freak. It has no related noun or verb. Webster's *New World* gives it as both adjective and adverb, but you should decide for yourself whether the adverb form wouldn't be *gingerlily*. And should you turn to *I Samuel 15:32-33* for the passage describing King Agag's delicate approach, be sure you use the King James Version. The Revised Standard translators say he approached Samuel *cheerfully*. It seems there's no end to the mistakes one might make with *gingerly*. So form your opinions gingerly. Or gingerlily. Or even cautiously.

'since'

(saved from a sinful ending)

The English-speaking human tongue has an unexplainable tendency to add a meaningless *s* to certain words.

You can see this ending, which often appears to be a pluralizing but isn't, in *anyways* for anyway, *backwards* for backward, *frontwards* for frontward, *towards* for toward, in *unawares* for unaware, and in *besides, crossways* and *sideways.*

Consider the word *while.* Originally it was a noun. It meant a period of time, as in "a short while ago." But the *s*-ending came along to turn it into *whiles,* which accounts for the still-surviving *whilst,* an adverb.

The same thing happened to *among* and *amid.* They became *amonges* and *amiddes,* the forerunners of *amongst* and *amidst.*

We also have this unfounded *s*-ending to thank for the present-day word *since.* The early Old English form was *siththan.* It was a compound of *sith,* "after" + *than,* a form of "that." *Siththan* became the Middle English *sithen,* which then picked up the *s*-ending and became *sithenes.* In time, the *th*-sound surrendered to elision and the word became *sienes,* pronounced "sins." To avoid confusion with the plural of *sin,* the soft *s*-ending was stressed deliberately hard, and "sins" ever since has been *since.*

Samuel Pepys, that lovable, clay-footed diarist, made repeated use of another word to which the *s*-ending had accrued. A glance at his *Diary* will show many entries beginning "Up *betimes...*"

It also will show that Samuel made repeated use of sin. Or, let us be open-minded, that sin made repeated use of Samuel.

130

'Japan'

(an English form of a Chinese word)

Japan officially consists of more than 3,000 islands which lie to the east of China and stretch from the Kuriles south to Formosa, a distance of about 2,000 miles. Four of these islands, Honshu, Hokkaido, Shikoku and Kyushu, are so much larger than the others and lie so closely together that, to the average person, they alone constitute "Japan."

To the Chinese, many centuries before Christ, this was the land where the morning sun seemed to rise. They named it *Jihpenkuo*, a Chinese compound meaning "land of the origin of the sun." *Jihpenkuo* eventually shortened to *Jihpen*, the name which the English-speaking people have converted to *Japan*.

The people who settled these islands gave them the collective name *Nihon*, now *Nippon*, a compound of *nichi*, "sun" + *hon*, "origin" — thus accepting the Chinese label which we know today as "land of the rising sun." The Japanese language, incidentally, is as different from Chinese as it is from English.

Nippon is recognized by the U.S. government as the official name of Japan, an identity which the American people probably will accept at whatever time the Japanese, or Nipponese, start shipping products stamped "Made in Nippon."

The names *Japanese* and *Nipponese* typify an interesting thing about languages. Very seldom is one language faithful to another language's self-designation. Or, to put it another way, very seldom do we call a foreign language by the name by which that language calls itself. Here are a few examples of *English* names of languages, compared with those languages' *self-designations*:

German	*Deutsch*	Lithuanian	*lietuviskai*
Flemish	*vlaams*	Russian	*russki*
Spanish	*espanol*	Breton	*breiz*
Welsh	*cymraeg*	Basque	*Euskara*
Albanian	*Shqip*	French	*francaise*
Greek	*Ellenika*	Croatian	*hrvat*
Armenian	*hayeran*	Danish	*donsk tunga*
Icelandic	*islenzka*	Polish	*polski*
Slovak	*slovensky*	Croatian	*hrvat*

| Serbian | *srp* | Sardinian | *sardu* |
| Indic | *Hindi* | Latvian | *Latviski* |

'spuds'

(and why the Ace of Spades
looks like the Ace of Spears)

Spudde is an obsolete English word that meant "dagger," in specific, and "sharp-pointed instrument" in general.

It came from the Old Norse *spiot,* which gave us the word *spit.* Not *spit,* expectorate — *spit,* spear, as in spitted or speared meat.

The sense of "sharp-pointed instrument" is found in the related word, *spade.* This explains why the Spade-symbol on playing cards looks more like a spear-head than a spade-blade. The Spanish word *espada* also attests to the kinship. It means sword.

The use of *spuddes* for spading, or digging, gave us the friendly old word *spuds,* potatoes. Now a slang-word, *spuds* at first was a provincialism, probably in some corner of Britain where potatoes were the principal diggings.

The meaning of *spudde,* tool, lasted much longer than that of *spudde,* weapon. Proving that the digger is mightier than the dagger.

'bull'

("a pistol in each hand and a sword in the other")

The *bull* in this case is not the male bovine, it's the *bull* of "shoot the bull" and "that's a lotta bull."

The Middle English form was *bul,* a derivant of the Old French *boule,* Latin *bulla,* meaning "bubble." The analogy is that of a statement so free of substance that it bursts like a bubble on the slightest examination.

As *bul* became the present-day *bull,* its earlier meaning softened somewhat, from that of deliberate exaggeration to that of unintentional mis-statement. It came to mean a clumsy and illogical "goof."

In this newer sense, *bull* applies especially to mistakes in writing, from which not even the giants of literature have escaped. For example:

> In *War and Peace,* Natasha in the year 1805 is seventeen years old. But by 1809 she has become twenty-four. In the same novel, Tolstoy describes Andrei's icon as silver, but later, by that alchemy known as *bull,* he turns it to gold.

> Dr. Johnson's *Dictionary* defines a garret as "a room on the highest floor of the house," after first defining *cock-loft* as "the room over the garret."

> In *Don Quixote,* Cervantes tells us that Sancho Panza sells his donkey, but without explanation Sancho soon appears riding the animal as through they'd never parted.

> Sir Walter Scott wrote of sunset in the east, and Dickens in *Nicholas Nickleby* has Squeers' poor little schoolboys hoeing the garden in the dead of winter.

By reputation, Irishmen are especially likely to make bulls. "As I write this," allegedly declared a member of the Irish Parliament in a letter to a friend in London, "I hold a pistol in each hand and a sword in the other." In admitting this Hibernian proclivity for bull-making, the Irishman Richard Steele concluded that the Irish air must be conducive to it, and added, "I daresay if an Englishman were born here, he would do the same."

But the most memorable bull of all belongs to an Englishman, Daniel DeFoe. In *Robinson Crusoe,* DeFoe tells us that Robinson awakens on his island to find that the wreckage of his ship has drifted in close to shore. Robinson excitedly strips to the buff, swims to the ship, climbs aboard, and happily fills his pockets with biscuits.

'oyster'

(so called because it's so bony)

The oyster hasn't a bone to its body, but it gets called "bony" just the same. Because of the hard, bone-like shell that encases it.

The Indo-European *oss*, "bone," developed into the Latin *os* and the Greek *osteon*. The latter provided *ostreon* as the Greek word for oyster. The Latin language borrowed it, changing it slightly to *ostreum*, which subsequently became the Old French *oistre*, English *oyster*.

Os is seen also in the Latin *ossifragus*, "bone-breaking." The *-fragus* ending (visibly akin to *fragment, fracture*) also terminates *saxifragus*, "stone-breaking." This is the origin of *sassafrass*, the name of the plant whose leaves made a "tea" once believed to be just the thing for "breaking" stones in the bladder. Although a failure as a stone-breaker, sassafrass later made a great comeback as the principal ingredient in root beer.

'bridegroom'

(in days of old, when men were brides)

Almost everyone who has given thought to the mechanics of getting married has wondered why the man in the act is called bride*groom*.

Most of them probably have decided that the meaning is "bride's groom," and let it go at that. Not her groom in the sense of one who combs her down, but certainly her groom in the sense of one who attends her, waits on her, looks after her. It makes sense.

But no.

In the beginning, there was no *bridgegroom*. Just two *brides* — one female bride and one male bride. The Old English word *bryd* meant anyone who was promised or spoken for, man or woman.

But since it was almost the woman who was spoken for, the word attached itself to her, leaving nothing for the man. And so a name for him was improvised. *Guma*, meaning male, was added to *bryd*, for *brydguma* — "male-bride."

134

But hold on.

Guma, under the abrasion of time and tongue, changed to *gome.*

With that mutation, *gome* became confused with *grome,* a word meaning "servant." In the confusion, *brydgome* became *brydgrome.*

Note that in Old English, the syllable *ome* was usually pronounced *oom. Rome,* for instance, was "Room," just as the *Domes*day Book was and still is "the *Dooms*day Book." *Brydgrome,* then, was *"bridegroom."*

As you can see, the word *bridegroom* should be *bridegoom.* Can you also see why it has never been corrected? That's right — men long since have concluded that the label of "servant" is a fitting one, and women in their infinite wisdom see no gain in discouraging such a conclusion.

'elope'

(just grab her and lope off)

The Old Norse *hlaup* meant "leap." It developed into the Middle English *lopen, loupen,* meaning to leap, to jump and run. You can see it in the modern words *lope, gallop,* and *interlope.*

And also in *bridelope,* the oldest English word for a wedding. This word, origin of *elope,* described the lope, or run, of a man bearing his bride to her new home — a ritual believed to symbolize the earlier physical carrying-off of the blushing bride.

Lots of old *bride*-terms have now been forgotten. The *bridecake* and *bridecup* were a wee snack intended to see a new couple through the rigors of the *bridebed.* The device we know today as a Maypole was once called *bridestake,* and a *bridewain* was a wagon bearing the hope chest. The term *bridal* derives from "bride-ale," the *brideale* being a drinking party for the two brides. (Yes, two — the groom at one time was also called bride — see *'bridegroom'* preceding).

Consider the word *bridelock.* Popular usage changed it to the present-day *wedlock.* Popular usage is a very powerful thing, but it has it limitations. Note that it changed only the *bride-.* It takes a court of law to change the *-lock.*

'reiterate'

(John inferred what Priscilla implied)

Reiterate is a prime example of popular usage's invincibility. Of those who use the word, it would be safe to say that 90% use it wrongly.

Reiterate doesn't mean "to say something again." That's what *iterate* means, from the Latin *iterare,* to repeat. *Reiterate* means to say again what's already been said again.

But 90% popular usage is pretty popular. The time isn't far off when *iterate* will be scrapped forever, and the dictionaries will give us only *reiterate* and tell us, with lexicographers' finality, that it means to repeat.

Another predestinate edict regards the pronunciation of *acclimate.* It is no more correct to say *ac-cluh-MATE* for *acclimate* than to say *ac-cus-TOM* for *accustom.* But popular usage long has been at work on this word, and several dictionaries already recognize both pronunciations. The day will come when they will recognize only one, the one which now is wrong, but which then will be correct. Meanwhile, Englishmen play it safe. They say *acclimatize.*

Popular usage also has made huge strides toward reversing the original meaning of *infer.* This greatly mis-used word has been greatly mis-used in even the highest places. A friend once elected himself president of the one-man *National Society For The Prevention of The Mis-use of the Word 'Infer.'* He sent out printed postcards to all those he heard mis-using the word on television, including Prince Philip, Jack Paar, Garry Moore, one of the Kennedys, and others who leave sizeable footprints across the sands of time.

This word *infer* is a term of communication, and communication is a two-pole mechanism. One pole sends a message; the other receives it. Sometimes the sending pole communicates *explicitly,* clearly and with unmistakable meaning. At other times it communicates *implicitly,* with vagueness or ambiguity which can be either intentional or unintentional. In the latter case, it *implies,* and the receiving pole must draw its own conclusion as to just what has been said.

This conclusion is the *inference.* It is the receiving pole's interpretation of the sending pole's implication or insinuation. It is not *sent;* it is *drawn.* When Priscilla Mullins asked, "Why don't you speak for yourself, John?," she *implied* something. John Alden, at the other end, did the *inferring,* drew the *inference.*

But popular usage would say that Priscilla *inferred* that she preferred John to Captain Miles Standish. Because of this popular usage, at least one major dictionary has assigned to *infer* an "alternate meaning" which makes it synonymous with *imply.* This is like saying that an alternate meaning of *receive* is *send,* but the best advice is "Don't fight it." It is sometimes excruciating to see the things we've believed in pass into disrepute and oblivion. But then, one always manages to accliMATE.

'caboose'

(it's the little red box)

All your life you've known what a caboose is, but you're one in ten thousand if you know why it's called a caboose.

The word comes from the Germanic, probably from the Middle Dutch *cabuse* or *kabuys,* meaning "cookhouse." The word earlier was *kabinhuis,* meaning the galley of a ship, which either derives from or is reinforced by *cabin aus,* "out-cabin," the name for the cookroom on the deck of merchants ships circa 1760.

Mencken suggests that the *-oose* ending of *caboose* was formed in this country, somewhat as we converted the Spanish *vamos* to *vamoose.* This is logical, provided that the term arrived on these shores as *cabaus* or *cabin aus.* Obviously, no such conversion would have been necessary, or possible, if it arrived as *cabuse* or *kabuys.*

This suggestion also tends to put *caboose* in the category of slang, which is not where it belongs. True, the identical spelling and pronunciation is to be found in the *Dictionary of American Slang,* but as a different word whose resemblance to the railroad *caboose* is purely coincidental. It is slang for *calaboose,* itself a Southwesternization of the Spanish-Mexican *calaboza,* meaning "dungeon."

A little Pennsylvania Dutch boy stood at a grade crossing with his mother, waiting for a long, slow freight train to pass. "Mama," he said hopefully, "when comes the little red box, the train is all, ain't?"

'Latin'

(or, how to be a great fool)

Saturn, or Cronus, as the Greeks knew him, swallowed all his children except one. His wife tricked him out of Jupiter.

When Jupiter grew up, he made Saturn cough up the others. They were pretty mad. Saturn had to flee and hide out.

He hid out in the Italian province now known as Latium.

Some say this is what gave Latium its name, i.e., it derives from the Latin word *latere,* meaning "to hide out."

Others believe Saturn innocent of such carryings-on, and argue that Latium derived its name from the Latin *latus,* "wide region."

The latter version probably is the correct one, but if you have any instinct for drama, you'll prefer the former. Either way, we can be sure that there is a Latium, that its early residents were called *Latini,* and that the language they spoke was *Latinus,* hence *Latin.*

Latium is the province in which Rome is located. Italy, at first, wasn't a nation. It was a collection of communities, everybody for himself. Nobody was more for himself than the Romans. They were very tough boys. In time, they whipped everybody in sight, and then went out looking for more to whip.

The more they whipped, the more important their language became.

Pretty soon the average Roman couldn't even understand a church service without it.

He couldn't understand law or medicine without it.

All the writing was in Latin, so he couldn't be a scholar without it.

In fact, he couldn't even be a very successful fool without it. As someone said, anybody can be a fool, but to be a great fool you have to know Latin.

'whisky'

(when in Scotland, spell it with an *e*)

After man invented wine, he yearned for something with a bit more octane to it. In time he learned that by boiling his wine, he could distill it into what we now know as *brandy.*

138

We have the Dutch to thank for the word *brandy*. They took it from their verb *branden*, meaning "to burn". For a while the name of the product was *brandywine*. Too much for the parched tongue, this soon was shortened to *brandy*.

The Romans had another name for it, *aqua vitae*, "water of life."

The Swedish took the cue for their notorious *aquavit*, also meaning "water of life," and the French followed suit with *eau de vie*, likewise, "water of life."

Not to be outdone, the Irish came up with their own life-giving water, which they called *usquebaugh*. In the Gaelic tongue they shared with the Scottish, *usque* meant "water" and *baugh* was a form of the Old Irish *bethu*, "life". (*Bethu* was related to the Old English *beon*, to be, to live, and to the Greek *bios*, "life".)

It isn't hard to see how *usque*, pronounced "oosky," became *whisky*. As for the *baugh*, it became *bae*, which explains Bobby Burns' line in *Tam o'Shanter*, "Wi' *whiskeybae* we'll face the devil." Later the *bae* went the way of *wine* in *brandywine*, leaving plain *whisky*. Or *whiskey*, as the Scots prefer to spell it. Spelled either way, it means "water". But neither the Irish nor the Scots have ever let this stand in their way.

'eeny'

(also 'meeny' and 'miney' – but how come 'mo'?)

"Eeny, meeny, miney, mo,
Catch a nigger* by the toe;
If he hollers, let him go,
Eeny, meeny, miney, mo –
Out – goes – you!"

Millions of us have grown up with this old children's counting-out rhyme, never dreaming that in a much more ancient

---

*This book means no disrespect to Negroes. In England, an early version of this particular rhyme advised, "Catch a tinker by the toe," and only a faithfulness to fact prevents that form being used here. The fact is that the rhyme is virtually unknown in this country except as repeated above. (Note: No disrespect to tinkers is intended, either, perish forbid.)

form it may have brought death to those who were "counted out".

It is one of many versions of ancient *scores* which possibly began as a way by which the Celtic Druids chose their human sacrifices. This must be said with qualification, for the evidence that the counting ritual was used for this macabre purpose is as vague as it is undismissable.

We do know that whatever their origin, there were in early England numerous semi-rhyming scores by which shepherds traditionally counted their sheep, old women their knitting-stitches, and fishermen their catches. We know that there is a definite connection between these scores and the old Celtic numerals, which survive even more clearly in the Welsh language.

Children, more impervious to the customs of others who came to occupy England, simply kept on using the old Celtic numerals in their games, long after those numerals otherwise had passed from the language.

Understandably, they are responsible for many corruptions, and corruptions of corruptions, as well as uncountable innovations and improvisations, so that many versions bear only the flimsiest relationship to earlier forms. On the other hand, some of these scores have come down to us with remarkably little change. For example, this rhyme sent to the London *Daily Mirror* by a twelve-year-old reader in 1948:

> *Ya, ta, tethera, pethera, pip,*
> *Slata, lata, covera, dovera, dick.*

Also this one, "discovered" in 1946, in which a beginning resemblance to the "eeny, meeny" version is seen:

> *Een, teen, tether, fether, fip,*
> *Sather, lather, gother, dather, dix.*

In 1877, A.J. Ellis, of the Philological Society of Great Britain, labeled such traditional counting formulas *"The Anglo-Cymrian Scores"*. This was a reference to Wales and presumably the Cumberland and East Anglian districts of England, where varying pronunciations of "one, two, three, *etc.*," present a highly apparent relationship to numerous scores. For example, the two rhymes above in side-by-side comparison with the Westmoreland and Yarmouth Scores, *one* through *ten*:

Rhyme	Score	Rhyme	Score
ya	yan	een	ina
ta	tyan	teen	mina
tethera	tethera	tether	tethera
pethera	mithera	fether	methera
pip	pimp	fip	pin
slata	sethera	sather	sithera
lata	lithera	lather	lithera
covera	hevera	gother	cothra
dovera	devera	dather	hothra
dick	dick	dix	dic

There's other etymological evidence of the connection with early numerals. The Welsh *un*, "one", is pronounced *een*. In the dialects of Yorkshire's West Riding, Northumberland and High Furness, "one" is respectively pronounced *eina, een* and *aina*.

The *Oxford Dictionary of Nursery Rhymes* feels certain that if we had knowledge of *more* of the early numerals, we could readily connect other children's rhymes to them. "Hickory, dickory, dock". for example, relates to the *hevera, devera, dick* of the Westmoreland Score.

It's too bad we don't know more. *Eeny, meeny,* and perhaps *miney* we can account for. But the way it stands we just don't know no *mo.*

'guts'

(soon it'll be too sissy to survive)

Not many years ago the word *guts* was outrageous enough to be on Hollywood's taboo-list, and that's pretty outrageous. Today it's so sanitized by popular usage that Braniff International had no hesitation about advertising itself as "The first airline with guts enough to put a clock on each plane." Today, in fact, *guts* has lost so much of its earlier shock value that it's almost certain to wind up on the scrap-pile.

It takes no guts to make such a prediction. The pattern of doom has already been established by *guts'* predecessor, *pluck.*

Now so respectable that it's *passe,* the mere mention of *pluck* once sent ladies stumbling for the smelling-salts. It began as a butcher's term for the viscera of slaughtered animals, the part that was "plucked out," and it lasted only until *guts* became a nastier word and thus let it off the hook.

Guts derives from the Old English *guttas,* meaning channel or canal (but not related to *gutter*). It was well established, in the intestinal sense, by the latter part of the 18th century. By that time, *pluck* was slowly becoming less synonymous with *entrails* and more synonymous with *courage.*

Pluck, as it began its climb to respectability, probably was used first as pugilistic slang. The climb was a long, slow one. Sir Walter Scott referred to courage as "that article blackguardedly called pluck."

But the Crimean War gave *pluck* great currency, and in 1879 the *Illustrated London News* escorted it into polite society with the editorial accolade, "Yes! The British word *pluck* is the word to use. 'Courage,' 'bravery,' 'heroism,' are all too feeble."

And now *pluck,* last seen in the company of Horatio Alger, Jr., is itself too feeble. And *guts* is almost sure to be turned into the same pallid pasturage, as soon as a sufficiently shocking substitute shows up. As Ernest Weekley pointed out, when a low word loses it lowness, it loses "the primitive vigor" that was its reason for being.

Like forbidden fruit, forbidden words are the juiciest.

'wiseacre'

(who says there were three Wise Men?)

Nowhere does the Bible say there were three Wise Men. Matthew was the only Gospels writer to record this story. *Matthew 2:1* says:

"...behold, there came wise men from *the east to Jerusalem"*

— and then, ten verses later:

"...*and when they had opened their treasures, they presented unto him gifts; gold, frankincense, and myrrh.*"

That's all.

True, in other and later writings, the wise men were called by name, Gaspar, Melchior and Balthasar. But these are legendary writings, from non-Scripture writers who assumed that each of the three gifts was brought by a different Wise Man. There could have been two Wise Men, or there could have been twenty. Or, to be sure, there could have been three. Nobody knows.

The word *wise* has broadened away from the narrower meaning it had when the Bible was first translated into English. At that time it implied a gifted, somewhat supernatural wisdom, much like the kindred *wiz* in *wizard*. It is related to the Old High German *wizago*, "prophet," and to the Middle Dutch *wisseger*, "wise-sayer," or soothsayer. This latter word, a compound of *wiss*, wise + *seger*, sayer, eventually became the derisive Anglo-American slang-term we know as *wiseacre*.

As further evidence of the connotation of super-wisdom in the word *wise*, remember that the Wise Men of the Bible were known also as the *Magi*. This, the name of a Persian caste of priestly prophets or sorcerers, is the origin of the word *magician*, an equivalent of *wizard*.

'hello'

(and something good for wassails you*)

The word *hello* owes it existence to rabbit-hunting. It comes from the Medieval French *halloer*, meaning to pursue game with cries of *Hale!* This *hale* is a variant of *haro*, the key word in the

*With thanks to John E. Matthews, a Chicago advertising man who once used this pun both functionally and delightfully in an advertisement for Schlitz Beer.

early French expression, *crier haro sur,* to "cry on" the dogs in pursuit of *haro,* or hare.

The early English *halloo, hallo, hullo* and *hello* are all derivatives of *halloer.* They form the base for the noun *hullabaloo* and also for the American *holler.*

The greeting, *hail,* looks as though it might also be a derivative of *hale,* but it isn't. It comes from the Icelandic *heill,* a salutation betokening health, prosperity, general good fortune. *Heill* is seen in the Old English *"Far heill,"* which later surrendered to the familiar *"Fare well."*

Another Old English goodbye was *wes hal,* meaning "be whole, be in halth (health)." *Wes* was the imperative of the Old English *wesan,* "to be," and in *hal* we have the ancestor of both *whole* and *hale.*

The expression *wes hal* became the Middle English *wasseyl* and *washayl,* which developed into *wassail,* a drinking toast, "to your health." Note that the brew known as *ale* has no connection with the last syllable of *wassail.* But it serves nicely if there's nothing better at the moment. Fill the steins. *Wes hal!*

'fair'

(amelioration, pejoration, and proof that
English gentlemen prefer blondes)

Word meanings tend to change for better or worse.

The change for the better is known as *amelioration*; the change for the worse is *pejoration.*

The word *fair,* as in "fair sex," "fair-haired," is a good example of amelioration. Originally, it meant nothing more than "suitable" or "satisfactory." The meaning changed to that of "pleasing," and then, with the logic that a woman must be beautiful to be pleasing, changed again to that of "beautiful." Hence the term "fair sex," i.e., "beautiful sex."

Interestingly, *fair* then picked up a secondary meaning. Given their choice, British gentlemen preferred blondes (Richard Burton notwithstanding), and so *fair,* beautiful, came also to mean *fair,* blonde.

Some words have ameliorated, or bettered, more drastically:

Natural was once a common word for *imbecile*.

Success once meant nothing more than *result*.

Romantic once suggested *vulgarity, poor taste*.

Zeal, meaning enthusiasm, once meant *fanaticism,* and *enthusiasm* at the same time was almost synonymous with *violence*.

Pluck, as pointed out earlier, improved its original meaning of *entrails* to that of *courage*.

On the other side of the ledger, there are many words whose meanings have pejorated, or worsened:

Wretch, a scoundrel, was once a tender name for someone to be *pitied*.

Pedant, now meaning "a show-off," as in *pedantic,* once meant nothing worse than "school-master."

Idiot was once the word for a laymen, a non-professional, a private person, and *knave,* now a rascal, a rogue, once meant nothing more defamatory than "boy, young servant."

Cunning, once meaning skillful, now means sly, tricky. That criminal rascal known as the *villain* was once only an humble peasant, while a *notorious* person was a well known, even notable person, and one who was *officious* was merely obliging.

Disinterested meant "impartial," and *obnoxious,* now meaning "despicable, *poisonous*," originally meant "vulnerable, exposed to harm."

Many word meanings have altered without bettering *or* worsening. For example:

Large once meant generous, liberal, as in *largess*.

Great at first referred only to size, later adding the meaning of *excellent*.

Preposterous once was just another way of saying "cart before the horse," i.e., *pre-post,* or "before-behind."

Flower was first spelled *flour,* a reference to the finer part of anything. We say *flower of manhood,* but *flour of wheat* has somehow remained unchanged.

Cry once meant any loud vocal noise, but today one who weeps silently is *crying*.

Stink and *stench* originally meant any kind of scent, good or bad, much like *smell* today, i.e., good smelling or bad smelling (although the noun *smell* would probably worsen quickly, to mean an offensive odor, if it weren't for the verb *smell*, which has no adequate synonym and which, by remaining respectable itself, keeps the noun respectable also).

Chaucer and Shakespeare used *sad* to mean calm, serious. The word also was once a verb — "to sad" was to press down, hence the term, *sad-iron.*

Read at one time meant only to guess, a connotation revealed in its kinship to *riddle.* Even today we "take a reading" to make an estimate, or — poor souls — go to a fortune-teller for "a reading."

When the meaning of a word changes, for better or for worse, there is nothing to be done about it. The flow of language is like the flow of lava; it goes where it wishes when it wishes, unheeding and unhinderable. The most useless thing we can do is cling to the original or "real" meaning of a word that has strayed from its nativity. It is easier to buy a blonde wig than to convince Englishmen that *fair* means nothing more than satisfactory.

'pun'

(Swift was a bilingual paronomaniac)

Words such as *pear, pair* and *pare* are called *paronyms,* no pun intended. Paronyms are the very life-blood of *paronomasia,* the art, if art it be, of punning.

The word *pun* is a clipped form of *punnet.* In turn, *punnet* is believed to have come from the Italian *puntiglio,* a fine point or quibble. *Pun* refers to the humorous use or mis-use of words which sound identical but, if one wants to quibble about it, have different meanings. The celebrated Jonathan Swift is one of history's most notorious punsters, possibly second only to Bennett Cerf. He could pun not only in prose, not only in rhyme, but even in *bi-lingual* rhyme. Here's an example of his work:

> *Mollis abuti* (Moll is a beauty)
> *Has an acuti* (has an acute eye)
> *No lasso finis* (No lass so fine as)
> *Molli divinis* (Molly divine is).

This may not be the best punning you've seen, but you'll have to admit you've seen verse.

'gun'

(be sure your search warrant is round-trip)

Men feel an intimate relationship with their weapons, as demonstrated by the custom of giving them female names. "Ol' Betsy" for a shotgun, sometimes for a rifle or pistol, is a familiar example. So is "Big Bertha", or *die dicke Bertha,* as the Germans called their famous World War I cannon. (For Bertha Krupp, wife of the German munitions-maker).

An earlier example is "Mons Meg". Made at Mons in Flanders (Belgium), "Meg" was a famous cannon in Edinburgh Castle. It may have influenced "Roaring Meg", the pet-name for a cannon which the Fishmongers of London gave to the city in the 18th century. At one time *roaring meg* was a popular name for any large and loud artillery.

But the most noteworthy of all such pet-names for weapons is *Gunhilda,* the Scandinavian personal name whose first syllable probably is the origin of the word *gun.* It was first applied to the medieval stone-throwers known as ballistas. A 1330 inventory of Windsor Castle's firepower refers to one such ballista as "*Lady* Gunhilda".

It's possible, but not quite as likely, that the word *gun* derives from the middle syllable of *mangonel,* the Old French name for such stone-throwing mechanisms. *Mangonel* comes from the Latin *mangonum,* meaning "mangle," or "mechanism." (Note that any resemblance of this noun *mangle* to the warlike verb *mangle* is purely coincidental. The verb has an entirely different ancestry, coming from the Norman-English *mahangler,* "to hack or cut").

In either case, as a "lift" from *Gunhilda* or as a less likely derivative of *mangonel,* the Middle English *gunne* became the predecessor of the modern *gun.* A "revenooer" presented an Appalachian mountaineer with a warrant to search his barn. "Well, Betsy," the old mountain man said, looking at the shotgun in the crook of his arm, "that piece of paper says he can go in. But it don't say nothin' about comin' back out, do it?"

'palindrome'

(Dennis and Edna sinned)

A dromedary is a one-humped camel whose chief claim to fame is his ability to run fast.

That's his chief claim to his name, too. It comes from the Greek *dromos,* which means "running." You see the same element in *hippodrome,* the Greek word designating a place where horses run, and during World War I the British used it to coin *airdrome,* the place where airplanes "run."

What does all this have to do with *palindrome?* Patience, please. Palindrome wasn't built in a day. Next we must consider the *palin-* element of the word. It also is Greek. It means "turning back," i.e., going back over.

A *palindrome,* therefore, is a word that can be run backwards with the same result. Words like *toot, nun, boob, deed, wow,* etc.

Palindromes also can be whole sentences. Adam — allegedly — introduced himself to Eve with a palindrome, "Madam, I'm Adam." Had Eve been named Iris, she might have replied, "Sir, I'm Iris."

People who have nothing better to do think up all sorts of palindromes.

"A man, a plan, a canal — Panama."

"St. Simon sees no mists."

And then there's the sad but predictable story of a lady named Edna who goes out with three beaux to sing, dance, have a good time:

"Pat and Edna tap."

"Elbert and Edna treble."

But wouldn't you know it, "Dennis and Edna sinned."

'especial'

(not especially more special than *special*)

The Latin word *species* means "visible form, outward shape." It derives from the verb *specio,* "I look at." This same *spec = look* relationship shows up in many present-day English words, such as *spectator, spectacle, inspect, retrospect,* etc.

Specio also is the ancestor of *specialis*, which is the parent of the English word *special*.

The question is, since Latin gave us *special*, how did we come by *especial*?

Blame it on the French. They have trouble pronouncing words that start with *sp*. They also have trouble with words beginning *sc*, *sq* and *st*.

The French solved this problem by *prothesis*,* a forbidding-looking term which simply means "adding on at the front." What they added was the letter *e*, as in *especial*. This *e*, or rather, the sound represented by it, gives them a sort of lingual springboard to the remainder of the word.

Fair enough. But why *both* forms, with and without the *e*, in English?

In many such words, we drop the *e* at will. In others, such as *especial*, *special* we retain both forms because they've come to have different meanings, sometimes very slight, sometimes quite substantial. A *state*, for example, is hardly the same thing as an *estate*, and *spouse* now is regarded as a noun while *espouse* is a verb.

Some of the other words to which French has added the *e* are *estomac* (stomach), *etole* (stole), *etude* (study), *equerre* (square), *etable* (stable), *etage* (stage), *esprit* (spirit), and *etuve* (stove). There are many more but the time has come to *estop* (stop).

'woman'

(and why some wives aren't married)

Why does *man* turn female when preceded by *wo*?

It's a story that began when the word *man*, originally meaning *mankind*, assumed a second, narrower meaning, that of "grown male human."

As this new usage grew, the need for a companion word representing the female opposite grew with it.

---

*Not to be confused with prosthesis, which is a different kind of adding on. Artificial limbs, for example.

The problem solved itself with the Germanic word *wif*, which came into Old English from the Old Saxon tongue.

Wif, of course, is the forerunner of *wife*, meaning married woman. But *wife* at first stood for any woman of marriageable age, married or not. Fishwife, alewife, dairywife, midwife – these weren't necessarily married women, they were just necessarily women. Shakespeare's characters, you'll recall, frequently address women as "Good wife."

There's no matrimonial mandate upon even the word *housewife* – Webster defines it only as a woman who runs a home, with all the implications of management efficiency but none of the marital bed.

With the word *man* in its narrower sense standing for the individual man, as well as for mankind, the word *wif* rather volunteered itself for *wifman*, literally *woman*-man, as opposed to *man*-man.

In both *wifman* and its plural, *wifmen*, the *m*-sound assimilated the *f*-sound, and the pronunciation eased into *wimman*, *wimmen*. (The *f* here was pronounced softly, much like the *v* in *wives*, and yielded readily to the stronger *m*-sound).

Where did the *o* in *woman* come from?

Undoubtedly from those dialectal differences which caused uncountable variations in spelling and which are not always fathomable. Any attempt to ascribe it to "woe, man," are thoughtful but etymologically groundless.

'lady'

(what once was kneaded is now only needed)

In its infancy, the word *lady* meant "bread-maker."

It came from the Old English *hlaefdige*, a compound of *hlaef*, loaf + *dige*, knead. Thus, loaf-kneader, or bread-maker.

The change from *hlaefdige* to *lady* results from the tongue's various devices for banishing consonants that get in the way:

Say "hlaefdige," letting the initial *h* be silent – "laef-dee-gy."

Next, drop out the *g*, and you should have something like "lafedee" or "lafedy."

Finally, let the *f* go (it was pronounced like a *v*, easily assimilated by the following *d*-sound) and that's how a hlaefdige became a lady.

The word's masculine counterpart, *lord,* was arrived at by same process. The Old English word was *hlafweard,* meaning loaf-warden, or supervisor of the family food problem. Pronounce *hlafweard* without the *h* and the *f* and the result is something like "laward," hence *lord.*

In the 18th century a lady named Mary Wollstonecraft wrote that all women yearn for ladyhood, and then defined that status as "simply to have nothing to do." This seems to have some relationship to *loaf.* Also to the needing of dough, a pardonable pun if there ever was one. But discretion is the better part of valor, and any hlafweard who makes such a suggestion should be prepared to back down from it, or better still, to deny vigorously that he ever made it.

'OZ'

(Puzzle: where did the *z* come from?)

In Latin, *duo* (two) + *decem* (ten) = *duodecim* (twelve).

Hence the word *duodecimal,* which describes the old Roman custom of measuring things by twelfths. Twelve inches to the foot, twelve months to the year, twelve anythings to the dozen, twelve ounces to the troy pound, etc.

The Latin word for this traditional one-twelfth was *uncia,* probably from *unus,* "unit." *Uncia* fathered the Old French *unce,* meaning one-twelfth pound, and Middle English borrowed the word intact. Later, the French substituted *o* for *u,* converting *unce* to *once.* This influenced a change in the Middle English word, but instead of replacing the *u,* the *o* simply joined it — *o* + *unce* = *ounce.*

Uncia also is the Latin ancestor of the Old English *ynce,* Middle English *unche, inche,* modern English *inch.* The word *uncial,* describing large, bold handwriting, has the literal meaning, "inch-high."

Whether we're referring to the *troy* ounce or the *avoirdupois* ounce, the abbreviation is *oz.* Everybody knows that. But what nobody can account for is the presence of the *z.* One theory is that it was picked up from the Spanish *onza.* This is at best an even-money bet. If anybody offers 3-2, poz. on it.

151

'lap'

(also *dewlap* and mountain *dew)*

Lap comes from the Middle English *lappe,* meaning a "fold," especially of cloth. A *lapel* is cloth folded back. When we sit down, our garments fold in such a way as to form a *lap.*

The loose fold of skin under the throats of oxen is called a *dewlap.* Here, however, *lap* is probably derived from a related word, *lobe,* meaning pendant flesh, as in *earlobe.* The element *dew* refers to the characteristic moistness of the dewlap. In Middle English, *dew* stood for moisture in general, but *specifically* that which exudes from any living animal body. This is not be confused with *mountain dew,* that living body from which the animal exudes.

'punctuation'

(Donnelly thought he had the goods on Shakespeare)

Before the invention of printing, men ran written words togetherlikethiswithnospacebetweenthemandnospacebetweensent- enceseitherinfacteverythingwasruntogether.

Some languages ignored vowels in the written word, a practice which is less shocking when we remember our own *mgr., rwy., tsp., pctg., slsmn., hwy., sgt., pvt., mfr., assn.,* and *hdqrtrs.*

Other languages in written form inserted a small mark, or point, to represent the missing vowel.

Greek manuscripts show that dots or points were used in writing for oratorical purposes as early as 185 B. C. But these were crude attempts at punctuation, so little-known and unappreciated that Charlemagne, a thousand years later, had to assign to scholars the job of reviving them.

Gradually, manuscript words were separated from each other, and sentences were terminated with various marks and points borrowed haphazardly from the old Greek examples.

But it wasn't until the invention of printing that punctuation of any methodical significance was born.

Although contributed to by many men, this first punctuation

system was due mainly to the Venetian scholar and printer, Aldus Manutius, in about 1500. It, too, made use of dots, or *points,* hence the word *punctuation,* from the Italian *puntiglo,* Latin *punctum,* meaning "point."

The Aldine punctuation was no overnight success. For many years, writers took all manner of liberties with it. Shakespeare's first works, printed more than a century later, show numerous crudities and inconsistencies in punctuation. And thereby hangs a tale, for it was this very erraticism in the Bard's punctuation that gave new flight, two and a half centuries later, to the old fancy that his works were really written by Francis Bacon.

This old accusation, known as the Baconian Theory, was first made public in 1769,* but it had never been proven, of course. In 1876, Ignatius Donnelly, a Philadelphia-born Minnesotan, thought he had found the proof.

Knowing that Bacon was interested in coded writing, Donnelly fancied that the hyphens, parentheses and italics in the first Shakespeare folio (1623) were the key to a Bacon code. Using these printed devices as "bases" for making forward and/or backward word counts, he could alight at will on any word Shakespeare had written, which he then rearranged into what he insisted was really Bacon's history of Elizabethan times. This theory — by which it might also be proven that Henry Miller wrote the Bobbsey Twins series — was elaborated upon and published by Donnelly, in 1888, in a 1000-page book which he called *The Great Cryptogram.* Absurd as his theory was, there is little question as to his original sincerity about it, and with malice toward none and charity for all we can assume that its implausibility is the child of one man's desperately wishful thinking.

Incidentally, Donnelly for six years was a U. S. Congressman. Wouldn't you know it?

'panderer'

(an immoral word with a moral)

According to Greek legend, which is as reliable as any other brand, Troilus fell in love with Cressida at first sight.

Troilus' father was the king of Troy, and with that kind of

---

*In *The Life and Adventures of Common Sense,* by the Englishman, Herbert Lawrence.

credentials he shouldn't have been very bashful with the ladies. But bashful he was, and as a result he had to send his friend, Pandarus, to tell Cressida what was on his mind. Cressida said it was all right with her, and she and Troilus then got together and vowed undying love for each other.

Centuries later, this story was immortalized by such men of letters as Chaucer, Boccaccio and Shakespeare. As a result of Shakespeare's version, *Troilus and Cressida,* there came from the name *Pandarus* the English word *pander,* meaning to procure female companionship for males. Or male company for females, if need be, one would suppose. According to Shakespeare, poor Pandarus called this bitter label upon himself, saying "Let all pitiful goers-between be called to the world's end after my name; call them all 'Panders.'"

He also said, "Let all constant men be 'Troiluses' and all false women 'Cressids.'" Cressida, you see, turned out to be quite a false woman. Somehow in an exchange of prisoners she was swapped for three Trojan princes and wound up in the tent of an enemy general named Diomed. Diomed was a very unbashful man. He didn't use any goer-between. Cressida got the message.

Troilus immediately started making plans to rescue her, but when Cressida heard about it she sent word saying forget it, she didn't want to be rescued. This was very unfair to Troilus.

Moral: faint heart ne'er won unfair lady.

'—ling'

(as in "chit'lins")

Chitterlings are pork intestines, scrubbed, sliced, and boiled for about half a day. Sometimes they're eaten boiled, sometimes after boiling they're fried until crisp. In the opinion of many Negro folks, who know them from old times as "chit'lins," they're quite a delicacy.

But contrary to general opinion, neither the dish nor its provincial pronunciation are Negro inventions. In England chitterlings were called *chitlings* and *chitlins* at least as early as 1848, and probably were eaten untold centuries before that.

154

The word *chitterling,* meaning "little intestine," is best explained as a corruption of the Old English *cwith,* which had the literal meaning of "womb" and was related to the Gothic *qithus,* "belly," and the Middle High German *kutel,* "gut." It gives us a prime example of the Old English suffix *-ling* at work.

This suffix, which had a Germanic origin, added the meaning "possessing the characteristic of," the characteristic being whatever the substantive indicates. For instance, a weakling is weak, a *foundling* is found, a *hireling* is hired. Within this same general meaning, *-ling* also was used specifically to form a diminuitive, e.g., *darling,* "little dear," *gosling,* "little goose," and *stripling,* "little strip (chip) off the old block."

There's another — *ling,* a homonymous suffix, whose origin is Balto-Slavic rather than Germanic. It probably comes from the Lithuanian *—link,* "a bending toward, an inclination." It's seen only in adverbs and its basic meaning is "toward," as in *darkling,* into the dark, and *headling,* headward, which since has become *headlong.*

Many people are revolted by the thought of eating chitterlings. This is understandable. What's not understandable is why those same people smack their lips over kidneys, liver, brains, raw oysters, and sometimes salted grasshoppers.

'dollar'

(made by money-making *lings* from the east)

In *Brittania,* his account of the British Isles from the earliest times to the late 1500s, William Camden wrote:

> "In the time of his sonne King Richard the First, monie coined in the east parts of Germanie began to be of especial request in England for the puritie thereof, and was called *Easterling* monie, as all the inhabitants of those parts were called *Easterlings,* and shortly after some of that countrie, skilful in mint matters and alloies, were sent for into this realme to bring the coins to perfection, which, since that time, was called of them *sterling* for *Easterling.*"

The respected Camden's etymology of *sterling* is probably folk etymology,* but this passage is interesting because the *-ling* in *Easterling* is the same *-ling* found in *chitlins* (see preceding). And even more interesting because it was these same Easterlings who played the leading role in the origin of the almighty word *dollar*. It's a story that begins in Joachimsthal, "Joachim's Valley," which was then so far east in Germany that it's now in west Czechoslovakia (where it is known as Jachymov).

Around the turn of the 15th century, the count of the East Germany realm known as Schlick began using silver from the Joachimsthal to mint one-ounce coins. These coins, called "Joachimsthalers" and sometimes "Schlickthalers," were of remarkable quality. They soon set a standard for coins minted elsewhere in Germany, and as they became less local, "Joachim" and "Schlick" were dropped from the names and the coins, wherever minted, were called by the surviving *thaler*. Remembering that the German pronounced *th* as *d*, it's easy to see how *thaler* became *dollar*.

Incidentally, the name *Deutsch* itself is the German pronunciation of the early *Teutisca*, "Teutonic," and *thal*, valley, pronounced "dahl," is a relative of the English *dale*.

'pay'

(the devil was payed, not paid)

The *pay* in payroll, payday, comes from the Latin *pacare*, meaning to satisfy, to make peaceful. The idea is that so long as a man gets his pay, he'll be peaceful.

If he doesn't get it, there'll be the devil to pay — but that's another kind of *pay*.

Pay is a homonym, one of those words which have the same pronunciation as others, and frequently the same spelling, but entirely different meanings. *Devil* also is a homonym. As a result, "the devil to pay" has nothing to do with placating Satan.

*(Philologists prefer the explanation that the word derived from the custom of stamping a small star into the metal to symbolize that standard now known as *sterling* (Old English *steor*, star + *ling*).

Nor was it intended to. "The devil to pay" is only half of the expression, as we see in Scott's *The Pirate* (1822) when Jack Bunce says, "the devil to pay *and no pitch hot.*"

Explanation:

The *devil* here was the name of the seam along the keel of a boat.

To *pay* the devil was to caulk it with pitch, or tar.

In olden times it was a great labor to get the largest boats, some of them small ships, turned up so the devil could be payed. It could be done only while the tide was out. Time couldn't be wasted, or the tide that waits for no man would return before the job was finished. You can imagine what happened when a gang of straining, sweating, swearing men got the devil turned up, ready to pay, and then found that somebody had forgotten to heat the tar. *The devil to pay and no pitch hot.* Some poor devil caught the devil.

'male' and 'female'

(even more different than you think)

Unconsciously, most of us assume that the *fe* in *female* somehow signifies an oppositeness to *male,* somewhat like the *wo* in *woman,* perhaps.

Actually, the words *male* and *female* have no relationship.

Male is from the Latin *masculus,* meaning "male creature." *Masculus* became the Vulgar Latin *mascle,* which went into the Old French and there shortened first to *masle* and then to *male,* after which the growing English language adopted it.

But *female* got its own separate start from the Latin *femina,* "woman." The *fe* in *femina* is the same as that in *fecund* and *fetus,* which, of course, are womanly matters.

Femina provided the diminuitive *femella,* a pet-form somewhat like "girlie" for girl. *Femella* went into Old French as *femelle,* which later went into Middle English with one less *l* — *femele.*

Male and *femele.*

You can guess what happened.

Looking and sounding that much alike, it was inevitable that *male* and *femele* would become even more similar. *Femele* lost little time in becoming *female.*

This story is a bit complicated, a circumstance to be expected where male and female are involved.

'he' and 'she'

(he was a he, but she was a that)

He and *she* seem to be related, just as *male* and *female* seem to be related, but actually they're unrelated, just as *male* and *female* are unrelated.

In Old English, the masculine personal pronoun *he* was just as it is today — *he.* But its feminine equivalent was *heo* — not *she,* as it is today.

She comes from an entirely different family of pronouns — the demonstrative. It traces through the Middle English *she,* earlier *sche, scheo* and *scho,* from the Old English *seo,* which was the feminine nominative singular, third person, of the demonstrative pronoun *thaet,* that.

Now you know what they're talking about when some delicious-looking *she* passes, and the boys on the corner groan, "Look at *that.*"

'time'

(and its tidy twin)

Many people know that the Latin expression *tempus fugit* means "time flies." This may be the reason for a common assumption that the English word *time* derives from the Latin *tempus.*

Actually, the English word has no relationship to the Latin, beyond the fact that they both derive, ultimately, from the Indo-European mother-tongue.

The Indo-European root was *di.* In the Germanic consonant shift, *di* was converted to *ti* (see *Foreword*), which then arrived in Old English as *tima,* the parent of the Middle English *timen,* meaning "to happen."

The Old English *tid,* Middle English *tide,* came from the same root. We think of *tide* as the ebb and flow of big waters, which it has come to mean. But it originated as a doublet, or twin brother, of *time,* with the basic meaning of "timeliness." *Tidan* meant to happen, to befall, to be*tide.*

It's easier to comprehend *tide's* basic synonymity with *time* when we recall such terms as *eventide,* evening-time, and *Easter-tide,* Easter-time.

The present-day word *tidy* is a form of *tide.* Originally it had nothing to do with neatness, cleanliness, but referred only to something seasonable, opportune, or, as we say today, *timely.* If this is news to you, it is a pleasure to bring the tidings.

'navel'

(an accusing eye fixed upon us)

"Though Buddhists regard it with fascination, obstetricians with respect, and belly-dancers as a way of life, no one not interested in finding the middle of his abdomen has ever paid much attention to his navel."

That's what *Time* said, and it makes you think.

What a fickle bunch we humans are. There was a time when we couldn't have gotten along without the navel, but as soon as it served its purpose, out to pasture we turned it. And there it is today, a small and lonesome martyr to the doctrine of *Whathaveyoudoneformelatelyism.* A solitary souvenir of the best connection a man ever had. Surely the time is high for paying some attention to this accusing eye fixed forever upon us, and this is an attempt, better late than never, to do just that. Etymologically speaking.

The word *navel* came into the language as the Old English *nafela,* a close relative of the *navem* of the Caesars, the *nabbhis* of Sanskrit, and many other words which trace through antiquity to the Indo-European mother-tongue. Its original meaning was "middle, central," and thus it came to designate that central spot on the human physique. This meaning is shared by the visibly related word *nave,* the central part of a church, also the center, or hub, of a wheel.

Admittedly, this kind of information puts neither rockets upon the moon nor money into the pocket. But remember it we must, as something long owed the navel. No spot on earth was dearer to our childhoods.

'world'

(and why Mr. Chaney was a werewolf)

Every time we see a map labeled *The World*, we see a liberty man takes with his language. The official name for this mortal coil is *Earth*. We live *on* the earth; the world is what we live *in*.

Consider the ancient Germanic word *wer*. It meant "man." Remembering the sameness of the *v* and *w*, it's easy to see the resemblance of *wer* to the Latin *vir*, also meaning "man."

Now consider another Germanic word, *oeldu*, meaning "age." It's the origin of the English *old*, also of *elder* and *alderman*. But originally it meant "age" in the sense of an entire life span, a lifetime, not just the latter years.

Wer + oeldu = weroeldu, the old Germanic compound meaning a lifetime, literally a "man-age." Gradually its meaning shifted from one of *time* to one of *situation*, the situation being that busy buzz of men known as *mankind*. In the meantime, *weroeldu* went to Britain with the Germanic Angles, Saxons and/or Jutes, and there developed into the Old English word *weoruld*. Say *weoruld* out loud a few times; it's easy to see how it became *world*.

And remember, of course, that *world* is properly the name for mankind, not just another name for Earth. We can be sure that when the Apostle John wrote, "For God so loved the world," he was talking about man, not this whirling chunk of dirt. After all, man, as it has been pointed out, is God's greatest creation. Although, as it also has been pointed out, nobody but man ever said so.

For the benefit of the late-show watchers, the Old English *wer* and *were* explain why Lon Chaney, Jr., with that shaggy hide and all those fangs, was pictured as a *werewolf*. He was a man-wolf, or as we say, a wolf-man.

160

'slang'

(it wasn't easy to be Mrs. Noah Webster)

Noah Webster defined slang as "low, vulgar, unmeaning language." He should have quit with "low, vulgar," which are at least debatable. As for "unmeaning," we'd be hard pressed to find words with quicker meaning than *baby-sitter, warm-up, comeback, sweetheart, dropout, undercover, playboy, backtalk, striptease, loudmouth, mama's boy, wallflower, go-between, hunt-and-peck, walkie-talkie, smoothie, milkshake, hitch-hiker* and *teen-ager*.

Slang is what keeps language from becoming a bore. It is a fountain of youth, perpetually splashing our vocabulary with new words — fresh, colorful, vigorous, sometimes humorous and frequently daring new ways to communicate. Most of these splashings run off or soon evaporate, but many of them soak in and become a part of the warp and woof of word-dom. Right now, there are slang words whose "low" origins won't even be suspected in later years, just as today there are words which — well, let's *see*. Here's a list of twelve well-known "legitimate" words. Can you spot the ones that come up from slang?

blizzard	furthermore	workmanship
until	clumsy	spurious
chum	fireworks	bump
nowadays	fun	strenuous

The answer is yes, you can. Blindfolded. All twelve once were slang — as were *hectic, devoid, recalcitrant, fretful, salary, hubbub, assail, sundae, blimp, wangle, hoax* and many, many more of our so-called "legitimate" words.

The word 'slang'

The word *slang* is itself slang, which is as it should be. We're not certain of its origin, but there are two proposals which are far more reasonable than any others:

1. It results from a coalescence in the expression, "thieves' language," i.e., "thieve*(slang)*uage."

2. It is a provincial past tense of *sling*, just as *slank* was once the dialectal past tense of *slink*.

Of the two, the latter is the more likely, especially when we consider that the Old English *slingan* meant "to twist." Also, the Norwegian *slengjenamn*, "nickname," and *slengjeord*, "slang-term," seem to be cognates of *sling*, and thus support this etymology.

The "thieves' language" concept, however, is not as remote as it might seem. The underworld has a traditional identity with English slang, thanks to a private vocabulary which sneakthieves, pickpockets, and street-beggars contrived in London at least 150 years ago. Even today, the underworld is one of the principal manufacturers of slang.

The birthplaces of slang

Slang comes from anywhere and everywhere, but its principal birthplaces are the underworld, the armed forces, the merchant marine, sports, show business, high school and college students, immigrants, musicians, the business world, hobos and tramps, narcotics addicts, and assorted trades and professions. This, of course, leaves little except the pulpit and the D.A.R. as non-producers of slang.

One automatic and bottomless quarry for slang is the clipped word — *specs, Sis, gas, jet, mike, prof, Coke, bus, doc, auto, fan, Miss,* etc. Few people recognize the slang origin of *varsity*, a clipped form of *university*, with the English pronunciation of *er* as *ar*, as in *clerk, clark* and *sergeant, sargeant*. Another kind of abbreviation gives us *awol, veep, snafu, veep, teevee, G.I., s.o.l., I.O.U., p.d.q., on the q.t., I.Q.,* and *deejay*.

Deejay, from *disc jockey*, is an example of slang that comes from slang. So are *mutt* from *muttonhead, bum* from *bummer, john* from *johnny-house, gate* from *alligator, mag* from *magazine, bunk* from *buncombe*, and many others, including *ham* from *ham-fatter*, a relic of the days when actors removed grease paint with the fat side of a meat-rind.

Portmanteau words, "carrying two meanings in one suitcase," are classified as slang, and many have earned a solid place in our national vocabulary. For example:

clash	(clap + crash)
flares	(flame + glare)
smog	(smoke + fog)
brunch	(breakfast + lunch)
motel	(motor + hotel)
blotch	(blot + botch)
travelogue	(travel + monologue)
sparcity	(sparceness + scarcity)

Linguists who speak of *true slang* mean *cant, jargon* and/or *argot* which has found its way onto the national lips. In reality, all these forms are slang, and it's hard to draw a line between them. Some modern dictionaries even define each of them in terms of the other two. There seems to be little need for separating them, but for those who feel the need, let's dismiss *argot* as tending to represent the same kind of slang that *jargon* represents, and proceed with cant and jargon:

Cant

This is the name commonly given to underworld slang, or "thieves' language." It's not intended to be understood in the overworld, but cant-words, thanks to newspapers and Hollywood, frequently go national and become true slang — *scram, fix, take the rap, stir-crazy, hophead, clipjoint, muscle in, rod, flatfoot, rub out, mouthpiece, gumshoe, bookie, take for a ride, hooker, mark, junkie, heister, frisk, cop a plea, pusher* and *punk,* for example. *Ice* is diamonds, *hot* describes stolen goods, *hijack* is to steal merchandise in transit, *shove the queer* is to pass counterfeit money, and a *stool-pigeon* is one who *squeals* to the *fuzz,* maybe *fingers* a *gunsel* who then has to *take a powder* to avoid the *hot-seat.*

The word *cant* is from the French *chanter,* to sing. As slang, it described the singy, whining utterances of street-beggars who also indulged in pocket-picking, pimping, and other petty privateering.

Jargon

Jargon is "shop talk" or "trade talk," the specialized lingo that belongs to uncountable trades, professions, and ways of life. Like cant, it's usually not known beyond its own circles of origin, but it sometimes leaks out, catches on, and becomes national or true slang.

The word *jargon* refers literally to awkward noises made in the throat. It comes from the Indo-European *gurg, garg,* the same root that gave us *gurgle* and *gargle.* It's related to the verb *gorge,* to fill to the throat. And probably to *gorgeous,* which is believed to derive from *gorgias,* the name for the ruffed throatpiece once worn by French dandies.

The jargon of the sports world has given us a great deal of slang, e.g., *pinch hit, behind the eight-ball, tee off, on the bench, toe-hold, struck out, sent him to the showers, in there pitching, in there swinging, threw him a curve, kickoff, grandstand, quarterback it, foul ball, call the signals, below the belt, in my corner, throw in the towel, blow the whistle,* etc.

The entertainment world has been exceedingly prolific. All of us are familiar with *stage-door johnny, Oscar, crooner, stooge, straight man, top banana, payola, Annie Oakley, belt it out, licorice stick, gut-bucket, swing, jazz, platter, upstage, emcee, $64 question, bald-head row,* and *make-up.* But there's a lot of theatrical jargon still unknown to the general public — *boff* and *boffo,* box-office hit; *brody,* a flop; *terpery,* a dance hall; *lobby professor,* an amateur critic; *mikemugger,* an actor who gets right on top of the microphone, and *sizzler,* an actor who hisses his s's. *Butter* is make-up, and *cheesecake* has its opposite in *beefcake,* the naked display of the manly chest.

And so on and on and on. It has been estimated that there are about 600,000 words in the English language (counting the hordes of scientific terms and combinations thereof) and that about 45,000 of them are slang of one kind or another. It also has been estimated that 20-25% of the average man's vocabulary is slang. Noah Webster may be whirling in his grave.

But *Mrs.* Noah Webster is the one to be sorry for. She couldn't even tell her husband she had a *run* in her stocking.

'buckaroo'

(and how to get rich)

Cowboy, meaning cow-hand, cow-worker, came into use in Texas about 1830.

Cowpuncher followed, some fifty years later, as railroads fingered out from Chicago and St. Louis in search of "the four-dollar cow with the forty-dollar market." Cowboys used prod-poles to drive cattle through chutes into railroad cars; they punched with the prod, hence *cowpuncher*.

They also poked with it, hence *cowpoke*.

Buckaroo was another slang term meaning "cowboy." It had a relatively short life and there are two interesting theories about its origin:

1. It came from the Mexican *vaquero*, "cowboy," which is the Spanish *vaca*, cow + *-ero*, the Spanish suffix of agency. The initial sound in *vaca* is a bilabial aspirant which the Spanish represents with both *v* and *b*.* Thus *vaquero, baquero* — and it's easy to see how *baquero* Americanized into *buckaroo*. "Yep. Cowpunchers," wrote Owen Wister in *Jimmyjohn Boss*. "Vaqueros. Buccaroos in Oregon. Bastard Spanish word, you see, drifted up from Mexico."

2. It derives from the Gullah word *buckra*, as Julian Mason insists in *American Speech* (Feb., 1960). Gullah is an English dialect spoken by Negroes who are descended from the African Gola tribes and who live along the South Carolina and Georgia coasts. *Buckra*, meaning "white man," Mason proposes, was used by Negroes in the American West as a derisive name for Mexicans who treated them as inferiors but who, Negroes felt, were hardly "white men" themselves.

Who is right?

Who knows, beyond doubt? True, there were about 5,000 Negro cowboys after the Civil War. But *buckaroo* seems to have been known in the West before that time. Mason feels that Negroes allowed the surface meaning of their *buckra* to be "cowboy," but it could hardly have had that meaning without the go-between *baquero* or *buckaroo*. As one man's opinion, *buckaroo* was already on the scene when Negroes arrived in the West, and they privately enjoyed its coincidental similarity to *buckra* and the

---

*For example, *Habana, Havana.* But by no means restricted to the Spanish. You occasionally hear the English *heaven* and *seven* pronounced "heb'n"and "seb'n." A child may reply "I habn't got it" when another demands "Gib it to me." Note also that the Latin *libra* becomes *livre* in French; that the German *haben* is the English *have;* that the French *chevalier* is the Spanish *caballero,* and that the Spanish *diablo* is the English *devil,* which frequently comes out "debbil."

double meaning it gave their word.

Cowboying, incidentally, is a very fine way to get rich. Look at Gene Autry.

'second'

(it's like making mincemeat)

How many clocks and watches in the U. S.? About 250 million? If so, they tick a total of 21 quadrillion, 600 trillion times a day. That seems reason enough for knowing why the time measured by these ticks is called a *second.*

Start with the word *minute.*

It comes from the Latin *minutiare,* meaning to cut into small bits, to subdivide *minutely.* Some of its kin-words are *minimum, minus, minor,* etc., all related to the business of diminishing.

The kin-word *mince,* meaning to diminish by chopping into bits, describes what happened when man decided to divide the hour into minutes and seconds. He minced it. Minced it in two steps known as "sexagisimal division," the dividing by sixty, or into sixtieths.

The result of the first dividing of the hour was called *prima minuta,* Latin meaning "first diminishing," *first minute.*

Then the first minute was divided by sixty, and the result was called *secunda minuta,* "second diminishing," *second minute.*

In time people stopped saying "first minute" and said just "minute." That was all right. But when they wanted also to shorten "second minute," they ran into a problem. They couldn't drop "second" without winding up with "minute" again. So they dropped "minute" and wound up with "second."

Incidentally, our word *miniature* is no kin to the above Latin *minutiare* words.

It derives from another Latin word, *miniare,* meaning to paint with *minium,* the vermilion once used to illuminate book pages. This transferred easily to the sense of a small painting or portrait, hence *miniature.*

Just think. Since you began reading this, our U. S. clocks and watches have ticked off a total of 22,500,000,000 seconds. This adds up to 700 years. Time flies.

166

'boustrophedon'

(the Greeks compared all three)

When we first discover that some languages, such as Hebrew, are written right-to-left, we tend to decide that one way's probably as good as the other, depending on what you're used to.

But is this so? Is there some extra facility in one system over the other?

The early Greeks must have thought so. At first they wrote right-to-left. Then they switched to left-to-right.

But not without trying a third way, a mixture of the other two ways. In some manuscripts, their writing proceeds in one direction to the edge of the sheet, then turns and proceeds in the other direction, back and forth, the way a field is plowed. For instance:

> Now is the time for all
> the to come to men good
> aid of their party. The
> jumped fox brown quick
> over the lazy dog's back.

The Greeks, reputed to have had a word for everything, had one for this system of writing. It was *boustrophedon,* from *bous,* ox, and *trope,* turn, and it meant "as the ox turns (in plowing)."

'mosey'

(fishermen wade and waders waddle)

Thanks to man's yen for the grass on the other side, the word *invade* now has a warlike countenance. But it hasn't always been so. Originally it meant only "to go in," from Latin *in + vadere,* to go.

The main element of *vadere* is visible in several English words. *Evade,* to go away from something. *Pervade,* to go through something. *Wade,* to go into water, is a first cousin, and from *wade* comes *waddle.*

Vadere, as you'd expect, shows up strongly in Romance languages. In the French *je vais, tu vas, il va,* "I go; you go; he, she, or it goes." Also in the Spanish *vamos,* "we go" or "let's go."

This Spanish verb form, *vamos,* came through Mexico to the American Southwest, where it produced two interesting American slang-words.

One was *vamoose.* There was a sense of urgency to *vamoose,* some of the meaning of "Beat it!" or "Let's scram!"

The other was *vamose.* It was more casual than *vamoose,* meaning to move along, to break camp, to be on your way. This is the origin of the slang-word "mosey." This familiar term, of course, always suggests a casual going, even a sauntering along, a strolling along. People seldom say they *mosey;* they say they *mosey along.*

In those days of Cochises and Pancho Villas and Billy the Kids, he who didn't know the difference between *vamoose* and *vamose* frequently didn't live to mosey. Along.

'cole slaw'

(made with a swollen head)

When Mark Twain said cauliflower is only cabbage with a college education, he could have added that the kinship extends to an even broader family of vegetables, all getting their names from the Latin *caulis,* meaning "stalk."

You can see the resemblance in broc*coli,* col*lards, kohl*rabi, *kale, cal* (Irish for "cabbage") and even in the *cole* of cole slaw.

Kool was the Dutch name for cabbage, and that might well have been the English name for it if the Old Picard *caboche* hadn't intervened. This French dialectal word, meaning "swollen head," went into Old English intact, later becoming the Middle English *cabage* and *cabbage.*

Slaw derives from the Latin *sal,* meaning salt. A dish of vegetables and herbs mixed together and seasoned with salt was known by the Middle Italian word *salato.* Its equivalent in French became *salade,* while to the Dutch it was *sla.*

Put *kool* and *sla* together, which is what the Dutch did, and you have *koolsla,* the origin of the English *coleslaw,* "cabbage salad."

168

'who' and 'which'

(God doesn't care which you use)

The opening of the Lord's Prayer is translated, "Our Father, who art in Heaven."

It also is translated, "Our Father, *which* art in Heaven."

The message will go through either way. God doesn't pay much attention to grammar. Grammar is the devil's department.

But there's an interesting reason for this *who* vs. *which* variation, a reason that takes us back to Old English times when *who* was *hwa* and *which* was *hwilc*.*

Hwa by the end of the Old English period or very early in the Middle English, had developed into *hwo*.

And then both *hwo* and *hwilc* were struck by what might be called "the big h-w about-face." Words beginning with *hw* were re-spelled *wh*. It made sense. If you'll say "hwat" out loud you'll see that it comes out "what," reason enough for the re-spelling. *Hwael* became *whale*, *hwerf* became *wharf*, *hweol* became *wheel*, *hwet* became *whet*, *hwistle* became *whistle*, *hwit* became *white*, and *hwo* and *hwilc*, of course, became *who* and *whilc*.*

At that time, *who* and *which* were interrogative pronouns, used only for asking questions. But *which* soon was given another job, that of a relative pronoun — a pronoun relating to a preceding noun or pronoun, as in "Render unto Caesar *that which* is Caesar's."

Who, on the other hand, had only one job, that of interrogative pronoun, throughout the entire Middle English period. It wasn't until the early years of the Modern English period that it began to function also as a relative pronoun. And even then, as such it saw rather spotty use.

This explains why the King James Bible (1611) translates the opening of the Lord's Prayer as "Our Father, which art in Heaven." People, not only those who did the writing but also those who did the reading, simply were accustomed to *which* as a

*The Old English *c*, as in *hwilc*, was pronounced two ways, depending upon the sounds adjacent to it. If they were back vowels, i.e., those pronounced with the tongue in the back of the mouth, *c* was pronounced as *k*. If they were front vowels, *c* was pronounced as *ch*. Thus *cild* was *child*, *ceosan* was "to *choose*," *aelc* was *each*, *swylc* was *such*, and *hwilc* was *hwich*, or *which*.

169

relative pronoun but not yet comfortable with *who*.

Isn't it a good thing God doesn't care about grammar?"Thou shalt not end a sentence with a preposition" would send more people to hell than the devil could put up with.

'naughty'

(there's nothing to it)

"He didn't care a whit."

This old expression means he couldn't care less, not much less, at least. In 15th century England a *whit* was "a bit, a jot, an iota, the smallest part or particle," so little that it was virtually nothing.

Which is an interesting switch, because before that its meaning was "thing," therefore *something*.

Originally in Old English, the word was spelled *wiht*. The *h* and *i* were transposed much later.

Now.

Just as we've compressed *no thing* into *nothing*, so did the Old Englishmen compress *na wiht*, no thing, into *nawiht*, nothing. If one says "nawiht" out loud a couple of times, he can readily see how the word came to be *naught*. The identical process produced *aught*, meaning "something": *a wiht* was compressed into *awiht*, now spelled *aught*.

Naught, nothing, survives as the common synonym for "zero," but it enjoys wider usage in still another surviving form, *naughty*. Originally, *naughty* described someone who did naught and therefore amounted to naught – a loafer, an idler, a bum. Today we say "he's a do-nothing" or even "he's a nothing," but in the old days they said "he's naughty."

How did *naughty* arrive at its present meaning? Well, we all know who finds work for idle hands to do.

What we don't know is why it's called work.

'yes'

(a far cry from the cry *oyez*)

In many Old English words, *g* stood for the consonantal sound now represented by *y*. For example:

Old English		Present-Day
geolo	*became*	yellow
gear	*became*	year
ge	*became*	ye
gist	*became*	yeast
geoc	*became*	yoke
gearn	*became*	yearn

Gea swa and *gea si* were two common Old English affirmative expressions. *Gea swa* meant "yea (it is) so," and *gea si* meant "yea, so be it." (*Si* was a present subjunctive form of beon, "to be").

One of these two expressions, probably *gea si*, eased into the single term, *gease*, which later took the form *gese*. Just as *gea* subsequently was respelled *yea*, so was *gese* respelled *yese*, and that's how *yes* was born.

When the Norman French went to England, they took along the custom of opening courts of law with the cry, "Oyez, oyez, oyez." The word *oyez* was the imperative, second person plural, of the French legalese *ouir*, to judge or "hear" a case. The cry simply meant "hear ye, hear ye, hear ye."

As Englishmen gradually came to minor positions in the Norman courts, some became court criers who, all along, had understood *oyez* to be, not French, but the English "O, yea." Accordingly, that's what they cried, modernizing it to "Oh, yes; oh, yes; oh, yes."

Whereupon the more knowledgable people, as R.B. Barham pointed out, presumably cried back, "Oh, no; oh, no; oh, no!"

'out'

(an outline of an outstanding outpour)

A man turns out, and if he doesn't chicken out, he might win out. Or at least luck out. But life is an all-out workout, and if he can't tough it out until he figures out how to make out, he will get left out, or miss out, or even get cleaned out.

Time out now, to point out that the word *out* is an outgrowth of the Middle English *oute,* which outlived the older form *ute,* from the early Old English *ut,* from which there developed *utter,* the out-moded form of *outer. Ut* is now petered out, but it's a good thing it brought out *out,* because we'd be out of luck at talking things out without *out* to help out:

We roll out, try out, sing out, hand out, wear out, cop out, rinse out, wash out, wring out and dry out. We eat out, check out, step out, beg out, bawl out, chew out, stick our necks out, back out and butt out. To get out of something we lie out of it, string things out, write them out, spell them out, lay them out, cost them out, act them out, and live in an outlandish outpour of outbreaks, outbursts, outlaws, outfits, outskirts, and even outhouses, though these are on their way out and found only at the outermost outposts.

We drive out to the ballgame; if it's not rained out we find out who's in the outfield, who can outrun, outhit, out-throw, outpitch and outcatch, who strikes out or flies out or grounds out or beats out a bunt, and who comes tearing out of the dugout to cuss out the umpire and get thrown out of the park.

We flunk out, cook out, blossom out, black out, stand out, bow out, crap out, hold out, fall out, pass out and — what's that? You have to cut out? Without hearing this out? Well, for crying out loud. Over and out.

'narcotic'

(and why neurotics add better than psychotics)

Zeus' wife, Hera, brooked no interference. When the little nymph, Echo, kept her from discovering which of the other nymphs Zeus was dallying with, she exacted a unique punishment. She made Echo speechless except to repeat what others said. Hence the word *echo.*

Echo was in love with Narcissus. All the girls threw themselves at Narcissus. Soon Narcissus was bored with all girls. He rejected even poor little Echo, who then went to live in a cave.

Another nymph prayed a rare curse upon Narcissus. She prayed that he who would not love others would fall madly in love with himself. When Narcissus looked into a pool of water and saw his reflection, it was love at first sight. He couldn't eat or sleep; he just sat there, numbly, in what the Greeks called a *narke,* a torpor, or stupor, until finally he expired.

This well-known etymology gives us *narcissus,* the name of the flower that sprang up where Narcissus died, and *narcissist,* meaning one who is sure he (or she) is fairest of all.

It also gives us *narcotic.* This word is a mating of *narke,* stupor, with the Greek suffix *-otic,* which derived from another well-known suffix, *-osis.* The latter, *-osis,* means "condition, state, process," and *-otic* refers to something in that condition, state or process. *Narcosis* is the state of stupor or numbness; *Narcotic* describes one who is under narcosis or something capable of producing narcosis.

These suffixes play important roles in numerous English words, e.g., *hypnosis, hypnotic; varicosis, varicotic; symbiosis, symbiotic; psychosis, psychotic; neurosis, neurotic,* etc.

There is an interesting difference between a psychotic and a neurotic. A psychotic thinks two and two are five. A neurotic knows two and two are four, but he hates it.

'coaster'

(the booze is still mobile)

That little round disc under the iced tea glass — why, of all things, is it called a *coaster?*

It's an interesting story, and it begins where you'd expect, with the word *coast,* which traces to the Latin *costa.*

The literal meaning of *costa* is "rib." Figuratively, it came to have a related but broader meaning, that of the side of the body. For example:

If someone approaches you from the side, he ac*cost*s you.

The friends who stand by your side are a *cote*rie (French *cote,* from Old French *coste,* both meaning "side").

The *cutlet* you have for dinner is named by an anglicization of the French *cotelette,* a rib or *side* cut. (*Cut,* here, is coincidental).

And *coast,* of course, means one *side* of the ocean.

But during the 18th century, *coast* also was common for the

173

side of a *hill.* Now you can see the beginning of "to coast." It's the modern form of the Middle English verb *costen,* a borrowing from the Middle French *coster,* Old French *costoier,* all meaning to coast down a hill, usually on a sled, hence "coasting."

Later, "coasting" broadened to include any vehicular movement powered only by momentum or gravity. Remember, during the Depression, when gasoline even at 19 cents a gallon was precious, and you sometimes "cut off the ignition and let'er *coast?*" Or when a bicycle was a *"coaster* bike?" You don't? Ah, youth. Well, then, surely you'll remember the "coaster" on your dining table.

The table coaster hasn't always looked as it does now. It once was much bigger, as big as a tray, in fact. But that's not all. It also had little wheels. It was used to pass the bottles at table. When someone found his glass empty, the coaster was shoved along and the wine coasted right up to him.

Today's table coaster, of course, has no wheels. But the booze, somehow, still gets around.

'river'

(world's second biggest trouble-maker)

There's only one reason why Minneapolis and St. Paul are two cities instead of one.

That reason is the Mississippi River which runs between them.

This is not merely a matter of physical geography. There's much more to it than that.

Consider the Latin *rivus,* which meant a river, a rivulet, a stream.

This word also had a very strong secondary meaning, that of *one side* of a river, one *bank,* one *shore.* This meaning is implicit in "Riviera," which has nothing to do with rivers but designates a part of the Mediterranean *shore.*

This one-sided meaning was extended by *rivalis,* a derivative of *rivus,* meaning "rival." Historically, people who live on one side of a river aren't too happy about the people on the other side. This relationship can range from a mildly competitive coexistence to blood and bombers — as witness the recent and still unsettled state of affairs along the Jordan. And that's why *rival* means what it does.

The old Roman *Digesta* of 533 A.D., which recorded the important words of ancient and notable jurists, refers to what it calls the "contests" that continually arose between neighbors over water rights. Right here in the U.S., as any hell-for-sart'in mountain man or cattle rancher can tell you, many a long and gory feud started as one of these "contests." And people have the same trouble all over, and always have, and probably always will. When it comes to making trouble, rivers and water rights are second to nothing. Except church choirs, maybe.

'spinster'

(and what Bakers should know about Baxters)

The noun-ending — *ster* is known as a suffix of agency, meaning that it identifies a person by what he does. A pollster takes polls, a punster makes puns, a teamster drives a team, etc.

There's another suffix of agency, — *er*. It's more common than — *ster,* being applied much more generally, to things as well as to people. A blinker blinks, a drinker drinks, a thinker thinks, a sinker sinks, and a winker winks.

There was a time in Britain when —*er* tended to apply to males and — *ster* to females. The man who baked for a living was a *baker,* but a woman of the same livelihood was a *bakester.*

In time, *bakester* came to apply to male as well as female. It was more common in the north of England and in Scotland, while *baker* was the usual form in the south. With the development of the surname system, beginning around the 11th century, *baker* led to the occupational name *Baker,* while *bakester* produced *Baxter.*

The same circumstances gave us the names *Brewer* and *Brewster, Webber* (weaver) and *Webster,* and *Deemer* (judge) and *Dempster.*

Spinster at first was only a female *spinner.* England's first big industry was textiles. There were many unmarried women who were employed as spinsters, and in time the word came to designate any unmarried woman of marriageable age.

There also was the word *seamster.* It became *seamstress,* influenced no doubt by the feminine suffix — *ess,* as in princess, sculptress, countess, actress, poetess, lioness, tigress, etc.

An upholder was a man who held up, or displayed, fabrics. His female equivalent was an *upholdster*. This is the origin of the verb *upholster*. To designate one who upholsters, the *— er* suffix was added to the already present *— ster*, thus *upholsterer*. The same did not apply to the tinker. The tinker doesn't tink, he tinkers. But just the same, he never became a tinkerer.

'get'

(something for the purists to get with)

After a man gets through work and gets home, he gets fed, gets the paper read, gets a few checks written and maybe gets a phone call. Then he gets sleepy. He gets undressed, gets his pajamas on, and gets to bed. He hardly gets to sleep before it gets to be morning, so he gets up, gets showered and shaved, gets dressed, gets fed again, gets the car out, gets back to the office and gets busy.

There are thousands of ways to use the word *get*, but the high priests of language scorn all except one. They say *get* (which comes from the Old English *geten* via the Old Norse *geta*) means "to acquire" and must not be used otherwise. God will punish them.

Idiomatically, people simply *get* everything. They'd get lost without *get*. For instance: get worked up, get calmed down, get hungry, get thirsty, get hot, get chilly, get wet, get dry, get wise, get tattooed, get offended, get acquainted, get sick, get well, get too much to drink, get sober, get rich, get robbed, get lucky, get sued, get arrested, get bailed out, get conviced, get pardoned, get hired, get fired, get fed up, get loud, get quiet, get technical, get tee'd off, get in line, get worried, get x-rayed, get mad, get scared, get silly, get taken down a peg, get the laundry up, and get whistled at.

We get going, get through, get in, get out, get used, get used to, get happy, get sad, get smart, get cute, get invited, get left out, get a move on, get nowhere, get blamed, get the last laugh, and get in our two cents worth about language purists who tell us there's only one way to use *get*.

'two'

If the English language hadn't dropped its inflected word-endings, as explained in the *Foreword,* today we'd be clawing our daily ways through a jungle of different forms of the same word, with strict grammatical rules about which form to use when.

Consider, for example, the simple adjective *two.* During the Old English period it had four different forms in the nominative and accusative cases:

Twegen (the precursor of *twain*) was the masculine form.

Twa was the feminine form.

Tu was one neuter form, but to confuse matters —

Twa, a duplication of the feminine, was also used for the neuter.

When the language shook off its inflected endings, gender no longer mattered. All nouns, pronouns, and adjectives became neuter. In the case of "two," almost as if by compromise the two neuter forms, *twa* and *tu,* resolved themselves into one form, *twu,* pronounced "twoo."

One of the important consonant changes of the early Middle English period was the loss of the *w*-sound in numerous words. This sound, when it occurred immediately before a back-vowel* or immediately after some consonants, especially *s* and *t,* was simply retired from active duty. For example, *ne wot (n'wot)* became *not,* and *swa* became *so.* Other words retained the *w* in the spelling, but dropped it from pronunciation. Thus *sword* took the sound of "sord," *answer* became "anser," and *twu* became "tu."

This accounts for the present-day pronunciation of *two,* but it doesn't account for the *o* in the present-day spelling. That's a little touch we owe to the early Norman scribes. When they came to England, they brought with them a new handwriting style. When this Continental script replaced the rune-like letters with which Old English had been written, a problem was born. Some letters,

---

*Made with the highest part of the tongue in the back of the mouth, as opposed to front-vowels, in which the reverse is true.

when they occurred side-by-side, tended to "run together" and confuse the eye. The handwritten *u* was an especially troublesome offender when adjacent to the handwritten *w, v, m,* and *n.* To solve this problem, the Norman scribes, when they found *u* in the company of these letters, began changing it to *o.* Examples of this respelling are seen in words such as *luve,* which became *love; sune,* which became *sone (son); cum,* which became *come,* and, of course, *twu,* which became *two.*

And that's how time and tongue took *twegen, twa* and *tu* and rolled them into *two.*

Many of our modern *"two-*type" words were born as compounds of the Old English *twa.* When compounded with other words, *twa* usually took the form *twi.* This accounts for *twilight —* the time of "two lights," those of the fading sun and the emerging moon. *Twin* is another example of *twi* at work, as is *twine,* two threads twisted together. *Twist* itself is a *twi-*word; with the meaning of "two strands," it produced the Middle English variant *twies,* which we know today as *twice. Twig* is shortened from the earlier *twigge,* which originally referred to the fork of a plant, the place where one branch became two. *Twixt* and *tween* owe their look and sound to *twi,* as does *twill,* a fabric made by doubling the warp threads. (*Twill,* incidentally, compares interestingly with *drill,* a three-thread fabric, from the German *drei,* "three").

There also were some noteworthy *twi-*words which are now obsolete. *Twichild* meant second childhood. A *twi-banked* ship was one with two banks of oars. A *twibill* was a double-edged bill (battle-axe), and *twiwifeing* was — that's right, bigamy.

The earliest ponderable ancestor of the word *two* was an Indo-European root which philologists say might have taken one or more of five forms — *duwo, dwuo, dwo, dwa* and *dwi.* This root is the origin also of the Latin *duo,* Spanish *dos,* French *deux,* Italian *due,* Russian *dva,* Welsh *dua,* and numerous other "twos." Through borrowings of assorted developments of this primitive root, the English language has enriched itself with words such as *duo, duet, double, dozen, deuce, diety, duplex, demitasse,* etc.

The resemblance of all these *"d-*root" words to the Old English *twa-* and *twi-*words becomes much clearer when we remember that Old English was a Germanic language, and that the Germanic traditionally converted the Indo-European *d* into the sound of *t.*

(There was another consonant shift, much later, in which the Germanic *t* sometimes took the sound of *z*, which explains how *twei* became *zwei*, the modern German word for "two").

'nanny'

(a sister of *nun*)

Why are those old family retainers who look after the children, especially in England, always called "Nanny?" It's just another way of saying "Auntie," justified by the Sanskrit *nana*, Greek *nanne*, and Latin *nonna*, all meaning "aunt."

The Latin *nonna* is also the origin of *nun*. In this sense, Sisters are Aunts. But Brothers are *monks*, not Uncles. *Monk* comes from the Old English *munuc*, a development of the Latin-Greek *monakhos*, meaning "solitary," which itself comes from the Greek *monos*, "alone."

'son'

(without a synonym to its name)

Tell a friend there's no synonym for *son*, and you can see the wheels spinning in his head. But he won't find one. Not even if he turns to the more liberal thesauri, for they'll offer only such "comparables" as *boy*, *junior*, *male-child*, *scion*, *heir* and *descendant*, none of which necessarily means "son," and some of which aren't even necessarily male. As for the more discriminating references, such as Webster's *Dictionary of Synonyms* and Crabb's *English Synonyms*, they don't even list the word.

Son comes from the Indo-European root *su*, meaning "to bear, to bring forth," and its derivative *sunu*, "son." *Sunu* prevailed through the Old English period, becoming *sone* in Middle English, present-day *son*. (For change of *u* to *o*, see "two" preceding).

Daughter is just as bereft of synonyms as *son*. The Indo-European *dhugter* led to the Old English *dohter*, *dohtor*. Middle English restored the *g* for *doghter* and later the *u* for *doughter*, whence the modern *daughter*. Now ask a friend to give you a synonym for *brother* and *sister*.

'map'

(and why tableware is flatware)

Because the early maps were drawn on cloth, *mappa,* the Latin word for "cloth," also became the Latin word for "map." A *mappamundi,* literally "cloth of the world," was a map of the world.

By the Late Latin period, *mappa* by dissimilation or other corruption had become *nappa.* This went into Old French as *nappe,* cloth. It remained unchanged in the French language, where today *nappe* means "tablecloth."

This explains several English words relating to cloth, all borrowed from French. *Napery,* for example, the general name for household linens, particularly those on the table. *Napkin,* formed with the diminuitive suffix — *kin* (as in *catkin, cannikin*), means "little cloth." The popular English word for diaper is "nappie." And from *napery* we derive *Napier,* a surname of the occupational class designating one who was in charge of the linens at a manor or an inn.

Here also lies the origin of *apron,* which started out as *napron* and lost its *n* to the preceding article, i.e., *a napron* became *an apron* (see *'nickname').*

Maps, of course, are flat. This characteristic led to another term meaning "map." It was *plat,* from the Greek *platy,* Latin *plata,* meaning "flat." We still use *plat* and its variant, *plot,* in the sense of "map."

The Latin *plata* was the forerunner of *plate* and *platter.* In French, *plate* is merely the feminine form of *plat.* This explains the modern term *flatware,* which originally designated plates and platters and now pertains to all table utensils. *Flatware* was just another way of saying *plateware,* plates being flat.

It also explains, less directly, why the ironing of napery is called *flatwork.*

That just about mops up the story of *mappa, mappa* also being the origin of *mop.*

'deer'

(for every *heder* there was a *sheder*)

The word *deer* was once generic for "wild beast," much as *animal* is today. It comes from the Old English *deor*, which was related to the Old Frisian *diar* and the modern German cognate, *tier*, all meaning "wild animal." During the Middle English period *deor* smoothed to *der*. A *heder* was a he-beast and a *sheder* was a she-beast. Spenser in *Shepherd's Calendar* (1579) used a variant spelling, *hidder* and *shidder*, which he defined in his glossary as male and female deer. Shakespeare, in *King Lear*, used another variant of *der* when he wrote, "Mice, and Rats, and such small Deare."

'shhhhhhhhh'

(and 13 other ways to spell it)

There are fourteen different English spellings for the sound of *sh*, typified by *sh*oe, is*s*ue, man*s*ion, mi*ss*ion, na*ti*on, suspi*ci*on, o*ce*an, nau*se*ous, con*sc*ious, *ch*aperon, *sch*ist, fu*ch*sia and *psh*aw. That's only thirteen. The other is *su*gar. Somebody once told Thomas Hardy that *sugar* is the only word that delivers the sound *sh* with the spelling *su*. Upon which Hardy replied, "Are you sure?"

'clean'

(what's so clean about a whistle?)

In its youth, the word *clean* invariably included the suggestion of smallness. Somewhat like *dainty*, perhaps; we never think of big things as being dainty, but we always think of dainty things as being clean.

Clean (Old English *claene*, Middle English *clene*) has many Germanic relatives. One of these was the Middle High German *kleine*. Its meaning was "excellent, fine, small." If this jump from the meaning of *excellent* to the meaning of *small* seems like a broad one, consider how the other meaning, *fine*, bridges the gap. It has the meaning of both other words, i.e., a fine day is an excellent day, and a fine difference is a small difference. You can see this ambivalence also in *fines* and *refine*, the fines of ore being both small and excellent, or high-grade.

This sense of refinement, of purity, gives *clean* a special kinship to the word *clear*. For example:

"Clean as a whistle" is an expression we've heard all our lives, but it undoubtedly is a twist of *"clear* as a whistle," which is the only way it's found in earlier writings. This clears up an annoying question for those of us who've wondered what's so clean about a whistle.

The synonymity of *clean* and *clear* existed at least as early as the King James translation of the Bible. The *Book of Joshua* reports that "The people. . .passed clean over Jordan." In other words, they *cleared* Jordan. The expression "clear my name" implies the *cleaning* of one's name, the removal of accusations, charges of guilt. Some of us say we "clean forgot"; others say "clear forgot." Some say "clear the table"; others say "clean the table off." And the pure-in-heart have both a clean conscience and a conscience that's clear.

'if,' 'and,' and 'but'

(three little very big words)

There are two theories about the ancestry of *if*.

The first proposes that it comes from an old Germanic noun meaning "doubt," in the sense of something not yet established, something conditional, something provisional, something "iffy." Supporting this theory, we have the Gothic and Old High German *iba*, Old Saxon *ef*, Old Frisian *ef* and *ief*, and Icelandic *ef* and *if*, all meaning "condition, provision, stipulation."

The second theory offers *if* as a shortening of the Old English *gif*, literally "gift," but in this case something *given*, or *granted*, e.g., *"given* my choice" means *"if* I had my choice."

Words, like names, can have more than one origin, which then come together because of coincidental similarities. Such might be the case here. If not, then don't sell *gif* short, especially when you know that its *g* was commonly pronounced as *y*, i.e., "yif." (A common enough occurrence — *see 'yes'*).

The story of *and* is simple.

It began as the Indo-European *ent* and *ant*, variations which survived through the Germanic prototypes *enti* and *unti*, into the Old English period when "and" was written both *end* and *and*.

It is possible that the *n* in these two roots results from nasalized pronunciation of *et* and *at*, i.e., *e(n)t* and *a(n)t*. This is indicated by the absence of *n* in the Greek *eti*, "moreover," and in the Latin *et*, "and." In Sanskrit, the root seems to have varied from *atha* to *ati* to *anti*, which had the sense of "in addition to."

The Germanic *enti* and *unti* are seen in the Old Saxon *endi* and *ande*, and, especially of significance to English-speakers, in the Old Frisian *end* and *and*, which Old English borrowed intact. In *unti*, you also can see the ancestry of the modern German *und*, and.

But comes from the Old English *beutan*. This word, a compound of *bi*, by + *utan*, outside, had the literal meaning, "by the outside."

(Note that *bi* usually took the form *be* when compounded with another word, as in *be*lief, which has the literal meaning "by-live," something one lives by, and *be*cause, actually "by cause").

Beutan, "by the outside" or, as we'd say today, "*on* the outside," had the sense of "other than," "except for." There is an analogy in the present-day expression, "outside of that," which we use to mean "*but* for that." *Beutan* smoothed into a later Old English form, *butan*, which then developed into the Middle English *bute* and the modern *but*.

'Dan Cupid'
(and that other master, Dan Chaucer)

"Dan Chaucer,
well of English undefyled,
On Fame's eternal beadroll
worthie to be filed."

So wrote Edmund Spenser in *Faerie Queene.*

But the reference wasn't to a Daniel Chaucer, it was to *the* Geoffrey Chaucer.

Dan is an obsolete English title, equal to *Master* and *Sir.* It comes from the Latin *dominus,* "master," as do the Spanish *don* and Portuguese *dom.* It's frequently found in poetry of the period, as in *Dan* Neptune and *Dan* Phoebus. And as in *Dan* Cupid, the little cherub who forgets his clothes but never his bow and arrow, and who is really *Sir* Cupid. Or, as millions of broken and bleeding hearts will admit, *Master* Cupid.

'surgeon'

(a professional handy man)

In his chronicle of Pilgrim life, William Bradford, governor of Plymouth Colony, described his friend Samuel Fuller as "a physition-chirurgeon. . . of great help and comfort."

Note that word *chirurgeon.*

It's an antique form of *surgeon,* and not quite as defunct as one might think. *Time* used it recently, in reporting the reception Rome gave the South African heart-transplanter, "Chirurgeon Christiaan Neethling Barnard."

The magazine also suggested that if the Romans were still building triumphal arches, they probably would have built one for Dr. Barnard and carved upon it, "Chirurgus Africanus Maximus."

Well, possibly.

More likely, they'd have carved *"Chirurgicus* Africanus Maximus." *Chirurgicus* was the Latin transliteration of the Greek *kheirourgikos,* a compound of *kheir,* hands + *ourgikos,* worker. A *chirurgicus* was one who worked with his hands – with the implication, of course, that they were very special hands for very special work.

This Latin word became the Old French *cirurgien* and *cirurgeon,* later *sirurgien* and *sirurgeon,* which developed into the Anglo-French *surgien* and *surgeon.* Although the spelling *chirurgeon* obviously was known in William Bradford's time (due probably to a Renaissance attempt to re-shape *surgeon* along Classical lines – see *'island'),* *surgeon* obviously prevailed.

'a' and 'an'

(and why *one* is pronounced "wun")

The Indo-European *oines* is the founder of a vast family of words meaning "one."

The Greek *oines* and early Latin *oinos*.

The later Latin *unus* and its feminine form, *una*, parents of the French *un, une;* Spanish *uno, una,* and other Romance equivalents.

The Gaelic *aon*, Welsh *un*, and Breton *eunn, unan.*

And from the Germanic root *ainax*, a host of "ones" including the Old Prussian *ains*, Old Saxon *en*, Dutch *een*, German *ein*, and Old Frisian *an.*

Especially the Old Frisian *an*, we might say, for this is the forerunner of the Old English *an* which has given us four modern English words:

(1) The indefinite article *an*, which for phonetics' sweet sake is used before words beginning with a vowel sound, e.g., *an* apple.

(2) The indefinite article *a*, which works best before words beginning with a consonantal sound (even *a union*, i.e., *a "yunion"*).

(3) The adjective *any* – from the Middle English *aeniy*, literally "one-y", to represent an indiscriminate quantity which, to be any quantity at all, must be at least *one*.

And, of course (4) the word *one*, from the Middle English *on*, itself from the Old English *an.*

The pronunciation of *one* as "wun" has been explained by one highly qualified source as the survival of a now-obsolete spelling with *w*. This is improbable. Spelling follows pronunciation, not pronunciation spelling. More likely, as another highly qualified source offers, this pronunciation comes directly from a Southern English dialect which handled *one* as "wun" and *once* as "wunce," just as it treated *oak* as "wuk" and *oats* as "wuts." How could this be? Dialect never needs a reason, it just happens. In this case, if it hadn't happened, we probably today would be saying *"onn,* two, three" and *"onnce* upon a time." And be just as happy.

'taxi'

(a touching story, especially on April 15)

The Indo-European word *tag* meant to take hold of, to seize, and in a sense to touch, as in "tag, you're it." With this meaning, it became the mother of a large and interesting family of present-day English words, most of which come through its daughter, the Latin *tangere,* a nasalized form with the specific meaning, "to touch."

Tangible, for example, meaning perceptible by touch, and *tangent,* touching upon.

Then there's *tang,* a touch of flavor.

Also *tango,* which defined a certain way of touching guitar strings long before it defined a certain way of dancing, and *contagious,* defining something that touches or attaches itself to something else.

The Indo—European *tag* had several variant forms, *teg, tig,* and *tak.* Through these, we can add to the family such modern words as *contingent, contact, intact, integer, contain* and *tactile,* all having to do with "touch." Also *attach* and *tack,* as in "tack on."

And, alas, *tax.* The Latin *tangere* produced a variant verb, *taxare.* It, too, meant "to touch," but it had a narrowed meaning, "to touch *roughly.*" (Or, you might say, to take someone to task, *task* being a metathetic form of *tax* — see *'nostril').* The concept of *taxing* as *touching* is seen in the common expression, "put the touch on him," meaning to extract money from him. And because of this, we have the word *taxi:*

Taxi is a shortened form of *taxi-meter,* or as the French say, *taximetre.* In Paris, long before there were motor vehicles, there were horse-drawn cabs. They were called *fiacres,* taking their name from the Hotel de St. Fiacre, the site of the first "cab-stand." These fiacres had meters hooked to the wheels, to measure the distance traveled and thus tell the driver how much to tax the passenger, how much to tag him, how much to touch him for.

It should be noted that *taxidermy* is only remotely related to *taxes,* having to do with an entirely different kind of skinning.

'love'

(and why some tennis players are seeded)

The tennis term *love* means *zero* in score, i.e., "love-all" means 0-0, "forty-love" means 40-0, etc.

Any schoolboy who has ever called a zero a "goose egg" will appreciate the explanation that this term *love* is a smoothing of the French *l'oeuf*, meaning "the egg." It's reasonable; words have far stranger reasons for being than that.

But serious dictionaries scorn such an etymology, usually by ignoring it. They explain instead that the concept of *love = zero* derives from game-playing without stakes, for *nothing*, for fun only or, "for love." This explanation is approximately as satisfying as the other, but that's all right — the danger lies in being dogmatic about either, especially when one has no better explanation to offer.

(There's another tennis term of which we can be more certain. It's *seeded*. Any tennis player can tell you that *seeded* refers to the careful matching of tournament players so that the best are not pitted against each other in the opening matches. But if he can tell you *why* it means what it means, leap the net and shake his hand. It takes its meaning from the way seed is sown, i.e., carefully distributed over the *whole* area. To *seed* tennis players in a tournament is to distribute the best ones over the whole list of contestants, to avoid matching the aces against each other, thus avoiding the elimination of too many of them, too early in the tournament).

The other word *love*, defining that power which makes the world go 'round, has an unexciting history. It began as an Indo-European word calculated to be *leabh, leubh* and/or *loubh*, which developed into the primitive Germanic *liub* and subsequently into the Old English *lufu*, Middle English *luve*, and modern *love*. To understand how *luve* came to be spelled *love*, see the preceding treatise on *'two.'*

'clock'

(look for the clue on your ankle)

The following list shows one word as it has been represented by ten different languages. Look it over, then see if you can decide what that word meant:

klukka	Old Norse
klocka	Old Icelandic
cloc	Old Irish
klokke	Danish
klok	Dutch
clugga	Old English
klocka	Swedish
clocca	Late Latin
cloke	Anglo-French
cloch	Welsh

If you say these words meant *bell*, you're right.

If you said they meant *clock*, you're hardly to be blamed, but wrong.

You see, the mechanical contrivances we call *clocks*, today, weren't even invented until almost the 14th century.

When they finally were invented, they were hooked to bells, thus reporting the hour just as the town crier had reported it with his hand-bell. The bell, in fact, was the only way they *could* report the time, because there were still quite a few years to go before they had hands and dials with numbered hours.

The significant thing about these new timepieces, then, was their bell, and "bell" became the name by which they were known.

The only thing is, *clock* was the name by which *bells* were known. Bells simply weren't called *bells;* they were called *clocks.*

Gradually *clock* became the name for the entire timepiece. This left no word for the bell, so one was recruited from the Old English *bellan,* meaning "to bellow, to make a loud noise," as in the bell (cry) of stags.

This explains why the pattern sometimes embroidered on socks and stockings is called a *clock.* It was never intended to symbolize the object we know today by that name, but rather the *bell* that was once known by that name. Today the hosiery "clock" is sometimes embroidered in the traditional shape of a bell, but more often it's a triangle or some other abstract of the bell-shape.

The bell-shape also is responsible for the name of that piece of millinery known as the *cloche,* and the *cloak* was named for the same reason, the way it covers the body, flaring at the bottom, like a bell.

Apologies are in order for suggesting, above, that you might find a clock on your ankle. Hosiery clocks apparently went out with bell-bottomed trousers.

'the'

(it has a lot of *that* in it)

The is the commonest word in the English vocabulary. Computers tell us that of the next 10,000 words you speak, 700 will be *the.* *

Because of this, it's hard to imagine an English narrative of some 18,000 words without a single *the* in it. But such a narrative is *Beowulf,* the oldest known example of English literature, and there's a good reason why *the* is so conspiciously absent from it. *The* is the English definite article, and the language had no definite article at the time Beowulf was written.

It did, however, have a need for one, and to fill it people turned unconsciously to the next best thing, the demonstrative pronoun *that.* This pronoun, declined in Old English through five cases in the singular and four in the plural, had three genders:

> *se,* masculine
> *seo,* feminine
> *thaet,* neuter.

Late in the Old English period, the form *the* developed. Its base was the *e* of *se* and *seo,* and its *th* was acquired through the

*The English vocabulary has at least 600,000 words, but according to three separate studies, including one by Bell Telephone, more than one-fourth of all conversation is composed of just thirteen words: *the, be, have, it, of, and, to, will, you, in, is,* and *that.* That's twelve. What's missing? *I* will give you one guess.

influence of *that's* numerous other declensions, all of which began with *th*. Thus it can be said that *the,* the word that distinguishes *that* thing from *any* thing, has a lot of *that* in it, both spiritually and physically.

'culex'

(if winter comes, can *culex*
be far behind, tra-la?)

Winter arrives officially each December 21, and then each dawn plunges us deeper into its chilly woes. Be of good cheer. Each dawn also brings us one day closer to Spring, after which the voice of the turtle will be heard in the land.

And after that, alas, the whine of culex.

As the preceding footnote says, the English vocabulary includes *at least* 600,000 words. The reason for the qualifying "at least" is that there also are several hundred thousand scientific terms which the man in the street seldom sees and almost never uses. He'd rather call *culex* a mosquito than call it *culex.*

Let it be said to *culex's* credit that he is only the backyard mosquito, not the one that gives you malaria. That's a job for his cousin, *anaphales.* Another cousin, *aedes,* is vice president in charge of yellow fever.

Culex has an unconquerable soul. We drain his homes and spray puddles and ponds with all kinds of chemicals. We plant minnows to eat his young. We dump Paris Green from airplanes, drive trucks up and down blowing poison into the air, and slap. But *culex* lives on. And what he lives on is us.

Correction, please. What *she* lives on is us. The male *culex* is a vegetarian. It's the female of the species that's after blood, and that may not come as any great surprise.

What this proves, of course, is that there is a scientific difference between things. Which is the reason for those several hundred thousand scientific terms at the seldom-seen end of our vocabulary.

'like'

If *only* is lonely, it's only because it's *one-ly.* Other than that, it belongs to a very big club, those thousands and thousands of adverbs ending in *-ly.*

By far the commonest of all adverbial suffixes, this *-ly* is a short form of the Old English *lic* and *lich,* meaning "like." It's the shortening that turns "one-like" into *only,* "quick-like" into *quickly,* "sweet-like" into *sweetly,* etc.

The word *like* seems to offer a different meaning when used to denote fondness, e.g., "I like it." But it only seems to. Even as a verb, *like* refers to a like-mindedness, a like-ness. In "I like it," the subject and object simply switch places, the true meaning being "it likes me," that is, "it suits me, matches my taste, agrees with me, pleases me."

Then there's the word *likely,* signifying probability of something "likely" to happen. At one time, a *likely* story was one eminently believable, quite probable. But *"A likely story!,"* said with tongue-in-cheek, has been said so often that the expression now means something quite improbable and eminently unbelievable. That word *likely* doesn't have the clearest credentials, anyway. It means "likelike," and that's not even in the dictionary.

'down'

(If it's Scotch, *doon* the hatch)

Dun was the Old English word for "hill." It survives today in *dune,* a sandhill, and in such English place-names as Southdown, North Downs, etc.

More usefully, it survives as the adverb *down,* from the Old English expression *of dun,* meaning "off the hill." This expression developed into the Middle English *a-dun* and *a-dune.* In southern England, the pronunciation was *a-down.* By the time aphesis did away with the *a,* the sense of the word had broadened from "down from the hill" and *down* had come to stand for any literal or figurative "down-ness."

The same meaning prevailed in the north of England and in Scotland, but there the pronunciation, *dune,* lingered on. Even today, more Scotsmen come *doon* the road than come *down* it.

Down is a much harder-working word than we realize. We give it little rest, forcing it into action even when we don't need it. We don't invite guests to sit, we invite them to sit *down.* We don't look at our feet, we look *down* at our feet. As the old song suggests, we don't even faw and go boom, we faw *down* and go boom.

We turn invitations and bedsheets down, turn down the corners of pages, and get down on our knees. We call people down, take them down a peg, cut them down to size, and talk down to them while looking down our noses at them. We kneel down, slim down, calm down, win hands down, hand clothes down, and sandpaper wood down. If we feel run down, we get a rubdown, or strip down for a doctor who writes down a prescription for something we can hardly get down. We are down on our luck, down in the dumps, down at the heel, and down at the mouth, but we survive, knowing that you can't keep a good man down. So drink a toast to the word *down.* Drink it down. If in Scotland, drink it doon.

'—kin'

(and other affectionate belittlements)

Language has a way of tacking certain endings onto nouns to denote something little, or something dear, or both. These are called diminuitives, pet-suffixes, and endearment endings.

The commonest is spelled three different ways, *-ie, -ey,* and *-y.* This is the suffix that turns *babe* into *baby, dog* into *doggie,* and *doll* into *dolly.* You find it almost endlessly in personal or "given" names, e.g., *Billy, Tommy, Hughie, Jeanie, Joey,* and it's just as visible in family names such as *Libby, Richie, Grady, Dewey, Rickey, Eddy, Hickie,* etc. Many surnames began as personal names.

Another very common pet-suffix is *-kin,* as in "lambkin," "honeykins," "daddikins," "sweetikins." This is the tag that turns a small cat into a *catkin,* a small can into a *cannikin,* a small man into a *mannikin,* and a small piece of napery into a *napkin.* When added to the "short"—forms of such names as *Henry, Thomas,*

Lawrence, and *Walter,* it produced surnames such as *Hankins, Tomkins, Larkin,* and *Watkins.*

Another once-popular endearment suffix was *-cock.* Englishmen still address friends as "old cock," much in the sense of "old pal," "old hoss." The term was applied to strutting, effervescent, cocksure or "cocky" youngsters, as somewhat the equivalent of the American "Buster." Like *-kin,* this suffix when added to the shortened forms of names, also created other names, such as *Adcock, Wilcox, Babcock, Hancock, Hickok, Leacock,* etc.*

Captain Henry Littlepage was commander of the Merrimac during the Civil War. Would you think that his family name has anything in common with that of the actress, Debra Paget? Thanks to still another pet-suffix, both names have the same meaning, "little page (boy)." This suffix was widely used in both England and France, as were *-ot, -in,* and *-on,* which also denoted "littleness" and which you see in *violin,* a little viol; *chariot,* a little carriage, and *marionette,* "little Marion." *Marion* itself is a diminuitive of *Mary,* meaning "little Mary." Here are a few examples of ways in which these three pet-suffixes influenced our family names:

"Rob" + *in* = Robin, Robbins, Robinson
"Col" (short for Nicholas) + *in* = Collins
Philip + *ot* = Philpot
Hugh + *et* = Hughet(t)
"Wilm" (from William) + *ot* = Wilmot
"Gib" (short for Gilbert) + *on* = Gibbon(s)
"Rawl" (Raoul) + *in* = Rawlins
Eli + *ot* = Eliot, Elliot
"Dob" + *in* = Dobbin(s)

*One contemporary writer on word and phrase origins says the suffix *-cock* means "descendant of." Names with that meaning are *patronymical* names, i.e., "names from the father." In English there are only two patronymical suffixes, *-son,* as in *Adamson,* and *s* with an implied possessive apostrophe, as in *Adams,* "Adam's boy." The suffix *-cock* describes the individual originally named, so names like *Adcock,* while they certainly are passed on to descendants, nevertheless do not mean "descendant of," and do not belong to the Patronymical Class of surnames but rather to another major class, that of Descriptive Nickname.

The short form, "Dob," above, is noteworthy. While "Bob" and "Rob" are the common short forms of *Robert* today, "Dob" was once just as common. So was "Hob." They account for such surnames as *Dobbs, Dobbins, Dobson, Hobbs, Hopkins* and *Hobson.*

Another personal name with now-obsolete short forms is *Roger.* "Hodge" and "Dodge" were almost as well-known as "Rodge," "Roge," and in them you can see the beginnings of *Hodges, Hodgson, Dodge* and *Dodgson.* You may recall that in *Canterbury Tales,* the Cook was called both Roger and Hodge.

'egg' No. 1

(which may egg you on to read *'egg' No. 2)*

"Schemers and flatterers would egg him on," wrote Thackeray, and to anyone who has grown up speaking English, there's no mystery about what he said. "Egg on" means urge on, incite. The question is, *why* does it mean what it means?

No great mystery there, either, once we understand that it has nothing to do with the noun, *egg.*

The *egg* we're dealing with comes from the Old English verb *ecg,* which itself is from the Old Norse *eggja,* meaning to sharpen, to put a point on, or to put an *edge* on. The idea of sharpening or pointing up someone's interest in something led naturally to the concept of "edging" that someone "on" – much in the sense of "nudging" him on.

Note the digraph *cg* in the Old English *ecg.* In Old English, every syllable was pronounced, so *ecg* at first was pronounced "ekj." Say "ekj" out loud several times and you can see how the pronunciation subsequently eased to "edj" or "edg." Thus, as spelling followed pronunciation, the digraph *cg* came to be written *dg.* In this way the Old English *mycg,* meaning "gnat," became *mydg* and *midg,* the forerunner of *midget;* in the same way, *brycg* became *brydg,* later *bridge;* and *ecg,* of course, became *edg,* later *edge.*

But before it took its new spelling, *ecg* produced a variant form. It was a shortening, influenced by the Old Norse *eggja,* to "eg, egg." This variant, still with the meaning of "edge," became the Middle English verb *egge,* and thus led to the expression, "egg on," to edge on or nudge on.

The Old Norse *eggja,* incidentally, was related to the Greek *aki, akis,* meaning "point, peak, sharp." This led to the Old French *aigre,* thence to the Middle English *egre,* which was the precursor of the modern English *eager.*

The relationship of *eager* and *egg* is pretty clear. To turn a fellow into an eager beaver, all you do is egg him on. Unless, of course, he's uneggable.

'egg' No. 2

("Certaynly it is harde to playse every man")

The English noun *egg* comes directly from the Scandinavian (Old Norse) *egg,* and we have no synonyms for it.

But before it took its unrivaled seat in the vocabulary, it had to get the best of a Middle English competitor which also meant "egg." This competitive word was a development of the Old English *aeg,* which itself was a relative of *egg,* having come from one of the Old Norse dialects. Here's the story:

As explained earlier (see *'yes'*), the Old English *g* was in many cases pronounced like the consonant *y.* Thus the Old English *aeg,* pronounced "aey," took the Middle English spelling *aey.* This shortened to *ey.* With the plural ending *-en* (the same ending that pluralized *child* into *children) ey,* egg, became *eyren,* eggs.

By that time the Scandinavian influence was hard at work, and the Old Norse *egg* had worked its way into English. For quite a while, the native *ey* and *eyren* strugged for survival with the imported *egg* and *eggs.* * *Ey* and *eyren* eventually lost out, of course, but not before the printer-writer William Caxton had an opportunity to record, in *Eneydos,* this delightful little vignette (in which the parenthetical additions are mine):

"And certaynly our language now used varyeth ferre (far) from that whiche was used and spoken when I was borne. . .In so moche that in my dayes happened that certayn marchauntes (merchants) were in a shippe in tamyse (Thames), for to have sayled over the see into zelande ("Zedland," southwestern England). And for lacke of wynde, thei taryed atte forlond ("fore-land"), and wente to lande for to refreshe them. And one of theym named sheffelde, a mercer, cam in-to an hows (house) and axed** for mete; and specyally he axyd after eggys. And the goode wyf answerde, that she coude speke no frenshe. And the marchaunt was angry, for he also coude speke no frenshe, but wolde have hadde egges, and she understode hym not. And thenne at laste a nother sayde that he wolde have *eyren*. Then the good wyf sayd that she understod hym wel."

To which good Caxton then added, wistfully, "Loo, what sholde a man in thyse dayes now wryte, egges or eyren. Certaynly it is harde to playse every man, by cayse of dyversite & chaunge of langage." He would be saddened to know that it is just about as harde today as it was thenne.

---

*"We also see in England," wrote Otto Jespersen in *Growth and Structure of The English Language,* "a phenomenon which, I think, is paralleled nowhere to such an extent, namely, the existence side by side for a long time, sometimes for centuries, of two slightly different forms for the same word, one the original English form and the other Scandinavian." Here are a few examples of English and Scandinavian terms, respectively, which have vied with each other: *no, nay; church, kirk; rear, raise; yelde, guild; shriek, screech; leap, loup; swuster, sister; ash, ask; yift, gift; shirt, skirt; from, fro.* And, of course, *ey, egg.*

**Metathesis — see *'nostril.'* (Also note that in the penultimate sentence, Caxton writes "a nother," a coalescence and metanalysis of "an other").

'hangnail'

(it's somewhat like *angina pectoris*)

By telling us that the mercer was "angry" (see preceding), Caxton makes him appear as a Terrible — Tempered Mr. Bang.

But that's not what Caxton intended. He's a victim of the same "chaunge of langage" he so wistfully laments. During the Middle English period, *angry* didn't mean what it means today. It derives from the Old English *ange*, Old Norse *angr*, which meant "sorrow, distress, grief, pain." The mercer, therefore, wasn't *mad* at the poor woman for not understanding his language; he was only *distressed*. It *pained* him to think that he wasn't going to get any eggs.

Ange, "pain," shows up in the present-day word *anguish*.

Also in that distress we know as *anxiety*, although this term is a Latin relative.

Also in the Latin-born *angina pectoris*, "chest pain."

And also in *angnail* and its variant form, *agnail*, from the Old English *angnaegl*.

What was an *angnail*?

It was that painful little shred of skin, over the root of the fingernail, that we call "hangnail" today. It was "angry flesh."

Without knowing what *ang* meant, folk etymology assumed that since the little flap of skin "hangs" over the nail area, *angnail* actually was *hangnail*. And so it has been ever since. But no great harm has been done. The hangnail needs only a label, not a definition. It has other ways of telling us that it is painful.

'omicron' and 'omega'

(and the English word *oo*)

The Greek alphabet has two "o's". One is *o-micron*, "o-little," and the other is *o-mega*, or "o-big."

Their difference is not one of size, or of capitalization. It's a difference of pronunciation. In Ancient Greek, the *o* called *omicron* took the short sound, as in *not*, and the *o* called *omega* took the long sound, as in *home*.

The two characters were written differently, too. *Omicron* was — and is — written just like the English *o*. *Omega* was written with two o's touching — ∞ — a graphic way of showing that the sound represented was long. Today, the *omega* is written as ω, a remnant of the two joined o's.

Alpha is the first letter of the Greek alphabet, and *omega* is the last. This is the basis of the expression, "from alpha to omega;" figuratively, "from beginning to end," or, as English speakers also say, "from a to z." This end-position of the *omega*, written ∞, led to an interesting but now obsolete English word, oo. It meant "until the end," or, as defined in Herbert Coleridge's *Dictionary of the Oldest English Words* (1863), "forever, always, aye." The Wyclif Bible used it in the translation, "I am alpha and oo, the begynnyng and the endyng."

The *micro* and *mega* elements are the Greek *mikros* and *megas*, "small" and "large, great." They are seen in numerous English words. We have *microbe, microfilm, micrometer, microscopic, microcosm,* etc., all pertaining to something little, and we have *megaphone, megalith, megascope,* and *megacycle,* all pertaining to something large, enlarged, or exaggerated. In medicine, a *megalociphalic* is a person with an abnormally large head. *Megalomania* is the delusion of greatness, often characterized by a passion for doing big things, or for exaggeration, or both.

'further' and 'farther'

(you can go only so *fur* with *farther*)

Further and *farther* are generally regarded as pretty much the same word. Some people think the difference was created to distinguish between physical distance *(farther)* and extent or degree *(further)*. Most people don't differentiate at all, but become regular users of *one* of the two forms for all purposes. The day may come when *further* will crowd *farther* out of the picture. Or vice versa.

Whatever popular usage dictates, so be it. It is very easy to be a yes-man to popular usage; no-men never can win.

But popular usage can change only the present and the future, not history. The historically interesting thing about *further* and *farther* is that as intertwined as they are, they came from different words. Related, no doubt, but different.

Farther is from the Old English *feor,* a cognate of the Old Frisian and Old Saxon *fer,* all meaning "far." The Middle English form of *farther* was *ferrer,* literally "far-er."

Further, on the other hand, is from *furthor,* the comparative of the Old English adverb *forth.* The verb form ("*further* the cause") was *fyrthr;* the adjective ("without *further* ado") was *furthra.*

Similar as they were in all ways, it was inevitable that *ferrer* and *furthor* should become even more similar. Which they did after *ferrer* came to be written *ferther.* (Remember the English pronunciation of *er* as *ar* — which, most incidentally, is how we got *varmint* from *vermin*).

Which form should you use for what?

It's correct to use *further,* which is both adjective and adverb, for *all* purposes — physical distance, time, quantity, extent, degree. The trouble is, many of the best educated people don't know it's correct. They've been taught that *farther* must be used for physical distance (which is the way you should use it if you use it at all). It depends, therefore, on whom you're with when you use *further* for all purposes. Emily Post says it's correct to eat chicken with your fingers, but that does you little good if nobody else at the table knows that Emily Post says it's correct.

'you-all'

(blame it on two Roman emperors)

Bergen Evans, a good man about words, says that many Southerners use "you-all" as a singular pronoun. God will punish him.

It's used when speaking *to* just one person, yes, but not when speaking *of* just one person. When Joe South asks John Dixie, "Did you-all go to the movies?" he's asking whether John and his girl friend, or his wife, or his wife and family, went.

Just the same, singular or plural, "you-all" is a funny way of talking. So, for that matter, are "youse" and "you'uns" and "yez" and, in some cases, "the both of you." But there's a perfectly good reason for them, and this is it:

The first person *I* has its *we,* and the third person *he* has its *they,* but the second person *you* stays the same, whether singular or plural. It's not always clear whether *you* refers to one individual or more than one.

But it hasn't always been this way. *You,* at one time, was just one of a team that lined up as follows:

Singular	*Plural*	
thou	ye	(subjunctive cases)
thee	you	(objective cases)

This system changed, and for the reason for the change, let's go back to those latter days of the Roman Empire when there were two emperors, one in Rome and one in Constantinople. Before that time, there had been only one Latin way of addressing one person. The word was *tu,* singular "you." But with two emperors, people addressing either of them began using the Latin plural *vos,* with the rationalization that they actually were speaking to a two-emperor team. With this, men wise to the power of flattery saw a new way to advance their own ambitions. They began addressing *any* man of any influence, any man who might help their personal causes, with the plural *vos.* Soon the pettiest of petty officials was no longer *tu,* but *vos.*

In the 13th century, this practice reached England. *Thou* and *thee,* which formerly were singular forms only, now were used as singular and plural, respectively, when addressing inferiors, children, and animals. Similarly, *ye* and *you* were used when addressing any superior.* With this, *ye* and *you* for some reason

---

*The two kinds of address were known as "familiar" and "polite." The familiar *thou* and *thee* became handy ways to show contempt for a person. Both pronouns produced slang verbs; to "thou" a person or to "thee" him, unless he was an inferior, was to insult him. In his *Diary,* in reporting the audience of a Quaker woman with King Charles, Samuel Pepys wrote, "She thou'd him all along." Quakers, of course, adhered religiously to *thou* and *thee,* and ran less risk of insulting even a king.

traded their respective subjective and objective places, but both remained plural forms. And so it was until about 1700, when *thou* and *thee* were dropped entirely. *Ye* soon followed them, and thus the field was left clear for *you.*

But, to get back to the problem, *you* by itself gave no clear-cut indication as to whether it meant one individual or more than one. Some people apparently felt the need for such an indication, and that's why "you-all," "youse," "you'uns," etc., were invented.

There was a time when singular verb forms were used with *you* to indicate that the "you" being addressed was only one "you." In a letter to Princess Anne, Queen Mary II wrote, "But seeing you was so far from it. . .," and John Churchill addressed his wife, Sarah, as "You who is dearer than all the world." Today, of course, *you* even when singular is always used with plural verb forms — you *are,* you *have,* you *do,* etc. The unbending laws of grammar do quite a bit of bending in this case. It's like a law saying we must stop on red at all traffic lights except one, and at that one, stop on green. A capital example of the way popular usage wraps grammar around its finger. But then, in language more than anywhere else, rules were made to be bent. The only language with fixed rules is a dead language, we-all should remember.

'apple'

(it told when something was rotten in Denmark)

One otherwise learned writer says that *apple* is the only English word for fruit that hasn't been taken from other languages. Pay him no attention. We can't dismiss that lightly the Old High German word *apfel.* Nor can we shrug off the unshruggable Eric Partridge, who suggests the possibility that *apple* comes from the Latin *Apella,* the place-name of an apple-rich section in Campania, Italy.

Whatever the ancestry of the word, the fruit is such an universal symbol for all fruit that its name shows up in the names of many fruits other than apples. That's a simple truth expressed in a complicated way that calls for some clarification. All right, in North Germany, for example, oranges are called *apfelsine* ("apple of China"), while the South Germans prefer *pomeranze* (from the

Italian *pomo*, apple + *arancia*, orange). *Pomegranate* is a Latin word meaning "apple full of seeds." The Greek *melon* means apple, and from it came the Early Latin *malum*, apple. There's a kinship in the Portuguese *marmelo*, quince, which eventually gave us the word *marmelade*. And, of course, there's *pineapple*. In fact, *apple* stands so universally for "fruit" that we can be pretty sure the Bible meant to tell us only that Eve picked a fruit, not to specify the kind.

The apple shows up in folklore all over the world. In Danish folklore, it was used as a chastity test. It turned pale when its owner was unfaithful. And that, we can assume, was —

The End

or,
as the
Revivalists
of Learning
would have
said, and
did,

Finis.

Index

· · S · ·

· · T · ·

· · U · ·

uncial, 151
upholder, upholster, 176
urchin, 47
-ure (oeuvre), 128

use, 68
used to, 68
utter, 117
u-v-w trinity, 43

· · V · ·

vamoose, 168
vamos, 168
vaquero, 165
v-b bilabial, 165
Vietnam, 77

virgin, 43
viz., 53
voiced/voiceless consonants, 4, 70
Vowel Shift, Germanic, 6
Vulgar Latin, 32

· · W · ·

walnut, 90
wasp (waps), 78
wassail, 144
wean, 67
ween, 67
Welsh rabbit, 89
wench, 41
werewolf, 160
wes hal, 144
West Germanic, 7
what, 18
when, 18
where, 18
which, 169
whilst, 130

whisky, 138
whit, wiht, 170
who, 18, 169
why, 18
wif, wife, 150
wiseacre, 142
with, 144
wittol, 37
wiz, wizard, 143
woman, 149
wont, 67
won't, 66
woo (wowe), 114
world, 160

· · Y · ·

ye (the), 69
ye (you), 200
yes, 170
yesternight, 113

yestreen, 113
Yiddish, 57
you-all, 199

· · Z · ·